ON THE SPOT READING DIAGNOSIS FILE

ON THE SPOT READING DIAGNOSIS FILE

Margaret H. LaPray, Ph.D.

The Center for Applied Research in Education, Inc.
West Nyack, New York 10994

© 1978

The Center for Applied
Research in Education, Inc.

West Nyack, N.Y.

Library of Congress Cataloging in Publication Data

LaPray, Margaret.
  On-the-spot reading diagnosis file.

    1. Reading--Ability testing. I. Center for Applied
Research in Education. II. Title.
LB1050.46.L36   428'.4'2   78-12125
ISBN 0-87628-620-1

Printed in the United States of America

ABOUT THE AUTHOR

Dr. Margaret H. LaPray received her M.A. from the University of Minnesota and her Ph.D. from Cornell University. She became a member of the San Diego State College faculty in 1957 and for many years served as Professor of Education and Director of Learning Difficulties at the San Diego State College Clinical Training Center.

Presently, Dr. LaPray is director of her own Tutoring Learning Center in San Diego and also teaches courses in reading education at State. She is the author of *Teaching Children to Become Independent Readers* (West Nyack, N.Y.: The Center for Applied Research in Education, Inc., 1972) and the coauthor, with Dr. Ramon Ross, of the primary readers in the Rand McNally "Young America Basic Reading Program." She has contributed several articles on testing and on reading to professional journals, has served as a reviewer for various publishers, and has appeared as a guest lecturer throughout the United States.

about this diagnostic aid

On-the-Spot Reading Diagnosis File gives classroom teachers and reading specialists at all levels 42 ready-to-use informal diagnostic devices for the *early* and accurate identification of individual and group reading needs. Each of these testing devices is thoroughly proven and is presented for easy reproduction and use, right on the spot, in reading instruction. Contents provide broad coverage of reading instructional needs, and testing levels span prereading through secondary school.

For quick access to test materials, the *File* is organized into eight distinct sections. Section I presents suggestions for becoming familiar with the various testing devices and for using them most effectively in your own instruction. The succeeding seven sections provide tests in the following areas: prereading (II, III), letters and words (IV), phrases (V), syntax (VI), paragraphs (VII), and attitudes and interests (VIII). Translated into terms of skill levels, these sections cover visual and auditory perception, developmental stages, reversals, receptive vocabulary, phonics (applied), comprehension and rate of reading.

As a help to the teacher, each section provides an overall introduction to the test materials in the section and their use in identifying and correcting difficulties in the particular reading area. This is followed by the tests themselves. Each testing device includes complete information for its most effective use:

Description: a brief description of the testing device
Appropriate for: students needing assessments in specific areas of reading or reading-related areas
Ages: the age levels for which the test is most appropriate
Testing Time: time required to administer the test
Directions for Use: step-by-step procedures for administering the test to an individual or group
Scoring the Test: directions for scoring the test and interpreting the results
Remediation: steps for taking effective corrective or remedial action

Most of the tests in this diagnostic file are meant to be administered individually. Although tests such as the Cloze, Maze, and Listening Tests may be given to small groups, or even to an entire class, individually administered they yield more information. Under individual conditions when the student makes an error, the teacher/diagnostician asks the student to think aloud. As the student explains his thinking it can be determined that the error was at the point of substitution or that it was a total misunderstanding of words correctly identified — two vastly different causes for a single error.

About This Diagnostic Aid

- It provides Listening (aural/visual) Tests for use at all levels.
- It emphasizes Teaching Needs Testing (TNT) focusing on the special reading instructional needs of each student.
- It presents broad coverage of reading development, from the prereading to the eleventh grade levels.
- It includes a Graded Word List and an Oral Paragraph Test, both of which contain the same ten graded words.
- It gives the teacher 42 ready-to-use informal testing devices that can be copied and administered right on the spot to pinpoint reading instructional needs.

NOTE: All of these testing devices can be reproduced directly from the pages of the *Diagnosis File* by hand or by machine for individual or group use within the classroom or school.

- It presents complete, step-by-step directions for selecting, administering, evaluating, and following up each diagnosis device.
- It includes devices for determining individual attitudes and interests related to reading.

Two brief tests that lead directly into the reading program are a Graded Word List and an Oral Paragraph Test, both of which include an identical set of ten words. In minutes, an individual student can be started on an independent reading level and on an instructional reading level appropriate to his assessed abilities.

Daily records of reading performance are an essential part of a strong reading program. Tests that are readily available and easily administered are invaluable aids in monitoring students' daily progress. Moreover, familiarity with a broad variety of tests at all levels results in greater sensitivity to students' needs and, consequently, leads to a more effective reading program.

Margaret H. LaPray

contents

Contents

APPENDICES

TABLES

SECTION I

how to use this diagnostic aid

(Contains "Test Overview Sheet")

This section should help you save time in putting the *Reading Diagnosis File* to most effective use in your own instruction. It outlines brief steps for becoming familiar with the overall content, identifies the learning styles and behaviors typically found in successful readers, and discusses the use of testing as a teaching tool.

Surveying the Aid

It is suggested that you first survey the *File* with a view to your own diagnostic needs. Familiarity with a broad variety of tests provides a strong diagnostic base from which to operate and, for this reason, it is advisable to use a definite procedure for totally exploring this aid. Many individuals find that a procedure similar to the following five-step sequence is of value to them:

1. *Search* totally by flipping through ALL of the pages, reading only snatches of sentences and paragraphs widely spaced throughout the work.
2. *Organize* a skeletal structure by pulling out guideposts to meaning and repetitive patterns.

    Guideposts:
    Title, Author, Copyright, Publisher, Preface, Table of Contents, Tables, Appendices, and Subheadings

    Repetitive Patterns:
    Introduction
    a. Description of Test:
    b. Appropriate for:
    c. Ages:
    d Testing Time:
    e. Directions for Use:
    f. Scoring the Test:
    g. Remediation:

3. *Read* once over lightly but without skipping pages.
4. *Evaluate* data you recalled as to its relevance to your own needs.
5. *Reread* selectively and in depth those sections directly usable in your own reading program.

Once you have surveyed the content of this aid, the next step is to become thoroughly familiar with the tests. Before administering any of them, you should study them selectively in any or all of the following ways:

- by reading the introduction to the section in which the tests are located.
- by reading all pertinent captions immediately preceding and following the test.
- by personally "taking" the test whenever feasible.
- by giving the test to a child for PRACTICE.
- by completing all data on a PRACTICE case — scores, error analysis, directions for remediation and, whenever possible, by extended testing.

For most reading programs, it is advisable to begin testing with the two basic entry tests: San Diego Quick Assessment and San Diego Quick Oral Paragraphs. Information gained from these two tests leads to subsequent appropriate tests. For example, Table I shows *San Diego Quick Assessment* results leading to other prereading assessments.

Table I
Prereading Assessments

Students unable to pass level RR[1]	Should be given: Test 1 — *Developmental Visual Perception* Test 2 — *Visual Perception/Motor Free* Test 5 — *Motor Development*
Students unable to pass level RR[2]	Should be given: Any of the tests for RR[1] plus Test 7 — *Personalized Reading Readiness*
Students unable to pass level RR[3]	Should be given: Any of the tests for RR[1], RR[2] Test 3 — *Visual Sequencing* Test 6 — *Reversal Letters and Words*

Table II provides an overview sheet listing all of the remaining tests in the *File*. As a result of testing the student on the San Diego Quick Assessment, you are given information which leads to additional tests dealing with words. And as a result of testing on the San Diego Quick Oral Paragraph Test, you are given information which leads to additional tests dealing with words in context, phrases, syntax, paragraphs and affective measures. (See pages 4-5.)

Learning Styles of Successful Readers

Before using these assessments, you should also give some attention to the combination of learning styles and behaviors typically found among successful readers. As tests are administered, observations should be made as to whether the child tested:

1. tends to be "reflective" with a need to succeed and therefore laboriously scrutinizes and mentally checks out the correctness of the answer before responding.
2. tends to be an independent worker and thinker; that is, does not wait for another child's response before answering.
3. tends to be "open minded"; that is, given the title of a book, he can see limitless possibilities for its contents.
4. tends to be oriented to print in a left-to-right direction.
5. is insatiably curious about letters and words and is continuously stimulated by billboards and other environmental media.
6. seeks out and enjoys looking at books and listening to stories of all kinds.

2

7. concentrates on listening to stories to the exclusion of noise and distraction.
8. seeks opportunities to visit libraries.
9. is responsible and not disruptive during library periods.
10. has a long attention span — at least in the area of reading.

Insofar as the examiner observes these actions in the child tested, such behavior matches that of most successful readers. While not all successful beginning readers have the ten behavior patterns outlined above, according to research findings, they have MOST of them. Conversely, non-readers tend to be impulsive, dependent, close minded, directionally confused, disinterested, prone to avoid books, lacking in concentration, unmotivated toward reading, disruptive, uninterested in listening to stories aloud, and have a short attention span for books.

Data from test observations will tell a great deal about a child's learning style, and additional information may be gathered from his or her present and/or previous teachers.

Extending Test (ET) Limits

Testing that involves *teaching* is a dimension often overlooked. Yet to some diagnosticians this is the most valuable measurement of all. Precisely how does a child learn in relation to interest, difficulty, repetitions, and time involved? Several tests within the *Diagnosis File* direct you to "extend" test limits. Extending test limits permits you to look intensively at the way a child learns on an immediate feedback and after a 20-minute lapse of time.

Testing that involves teaching is productive diagnosis. Durrell and Mills are among the few test authors to incorporate this feature in published tests. Durrell does this in his "Analysis of Reading Difficulty" in the section entitled *Learning Rate* "designed primarily for the non-reader or the preprimer reader." Words are taught and after a 20-minute interval they are tested. The Mills "Learning Methods Test" also focuses on the learning process.

In order to predict a student's ability to learn letter names, phonics, structure, and/or vocabulary, it is logical to extend testing procedures. Although impossible to build in "laboratory controls," some quantifiable measures are as follows:

- Number of items known
- Number of items not known
- Number of repetitions needed for immediate recall of new item(s)
- Ratio of items recalled to items newly presented
- Ratio of items known in delayed recall to items newly presented
- Depth of understanding — ratio of time to accuracy

The following sample testing/teaching sequence taken from the fifth-grade reading level of the San Diego Quick Assessment, Form I, illustrates extended testing (ET). The student is asked to pronounce each word:

Student Response	*Stimulus*
+	scanty
+	business
+	develop
+	considered
disgusted	discussed
behăve	behave
+	splendid
acquired	acquainted
escaped	escape
grin	grim

+ correct responses   Raw Score   5 out of 10

Table II
Test Overview Sheet

AGE	GRADE	SDQA GRADED WORDS #11-12	SDQ ORAL PARAGRAPHS 32-33	DEVELOPMENTAL 1-5	REVERSALS 6	READING READINESS 7	NON-VERBAL INTELLIGENCE 8	VOCABULARY RECEPTIVE 9	ENGLISH/SPANISH DOMINANCE 10	APPLIED PHONICS 13	STRUCTURAL ANALYSIS 14	WORD OPPOSITES 15	TYPICAL USES 16	WORD RELATIONSHIPS 17	WORD SETS 18	PHRASE LEVELS 19	PREPOSITIONS 20
5	kdgn																
6	1																
7	2					*											
8	3					*											
9	4			*		*	*										
10	5			*	*		*										*
11	6			*	*		*			*							*
12	7				*				*	*							*
13	8							*	*	*	*						
14	9							*	*		*						
15	10							*						*	*	*	
16	11		*											*	*	*	
17	12	*	*									*	*	*	*	*	

*May be given to students with learning difficulties or reading disabilities.

Extended Testing (ET) Sequence

A. Teach what is NOT known first:
   In this instance, the student was willing to TRY every word. If he had said "I don't know" for any of the words, these would have *been the first ones to teach*.

B. Teach the gross substitutions next:

Table II
Test Overview Sheet

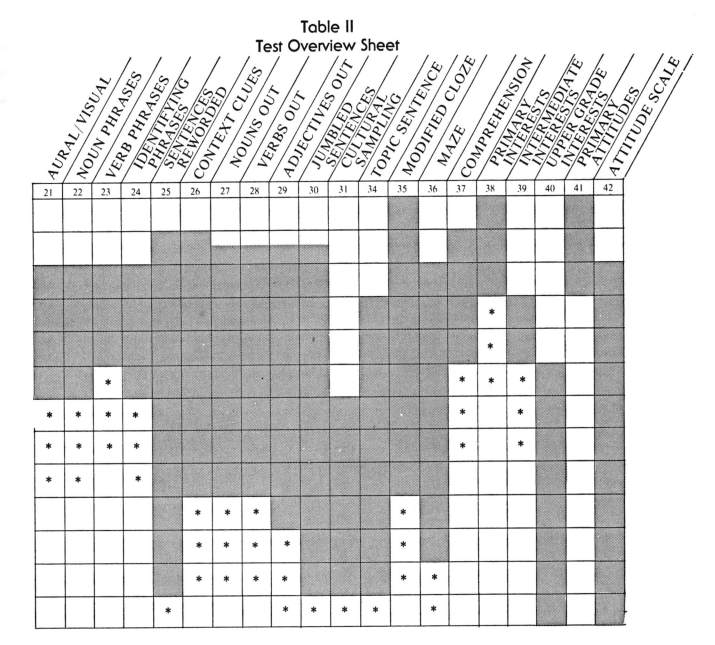

1. Correct the pronunciation: "You said *behăve* for *behave*. Part of the word looks like hăve but in this instance the word really has a long ā and sounds like hāve. Therefore, the whole word is *behāve*."
2. Use the Glass Analysis procedure:
   a. Teacher pronounces the word *behave*.
   b. Teacher says, "Which letters stand for *be*?...
      Which letters stand for *have*?"

    c. Teacher says, "What sound does the *b e* stand for?
       What sound does the *h a v e* stand for?"
    d. Student pronounces the word *behave.*
  3. Associate meaning:
    a. "Can you tell me the meaning of the word?" If not,
       supply the meaning.
    b. Ask for a synonym, antonym, or word category.

    behave:

mind or obey	(synonym)
disobey	(antonym)
mind, obey, use good manners	(word category)

C. Teach all other substitutions in a similar manner:
  1. Correct pronunciation.
  2. Use the Glass Analysis procedure.
  3. Associate meaning.

D. Present the words in the order just taught to test immediate recall.

    + discussed
    + behave
    – acquainted
    + escape
    + grim

Raw Score 4 out of 5

Tell the student any words he does not know. In the example, since he missed the word *acquainted,* pronounce it for him.

E. After approximately 20 minutes, retest in the order just taught.

    + discussed
    + behave
    + acquainted
    + escape
    + grim

Raw Score 5 out of 5

Compliment the student for his good memory.

F. Immediately following step E, retest in the exact order of the *original* testing to measure the student's dependence on word order.

    scanty
    business
    develop, etc.

Total Score 9 out of 10

The student's *set* of scores now looks like this:

Original Raw Score ....5 out of 10
ET Immediate Recall ....4 out of 5
ET Delayed Recall ....5 out of 5
Recall in original order ....9 out of 10

Although the student's original score was low — only half of the words were known — his prognosis is good. He responds well on a one-to-one basis. His delayed recall is perfect and his recall with the original word order is nearly perfect.

Not all ET responses will go as well. Had the teaching NOT gone well, a sensitive diagnostician would have dropped back to a lower level of word difficulty.

Extended Testing (ET) Guidelines

ET guidelines followed in the isolated word pronunciation test are:

1. Teach items only IF no more than ½ are incorrect in tests of 12 items or less.
2. Teach items missed beginning with those not attempted or with gross errors.
3. In teaching words missed:
   a. Follow a procedure of approximately the same time and sequence per item, to include
      *Correct pronunciation
      *Glass Analysis procedure for decoding
      *Associate meaning
   b. Teach the minimal errors last.
   c. Retest for immediate recall in the order just taught.
   d. After approximately 20 minutes, test for delayed recall in the same order as step c.
   e. Immediately after delayed recall, test the items in the same order in which they originally appeared on the test.
4. Record the student's SET of scores:

	Raw Score	*Total*
Original Raw Score	out of	
ET Immediate Recall	out of	
ET Delayed Recall	out of	
Retest Score	out of	

Diagnosticians need measures of a student's response to learning rather than a raw score. In most informal individual testing, "extending the test limits" may be the most valuable information the diagnostician gathers. Some record of the child's ability to learn in TIME, through REPETITION, by DECODING, and through changed word order is helpful. Capacity-to-learn measures are far more helpful in changing failure to success than a grade score, standard score, or percentile rank.

An easy source of ET-type testing is an informal test already in existence with more than one form. Note which test form has been used in an *extended* manner as a pretest. Use the alternate form as a posttest administered in a similar *extended* manner. In place of two raw scores to compare, you will have two SETS of student responses to teaching which include such measures as ratio of unknown to known, immediate recall, delayed recall, response to instruction, and amount of interference resulting from changes in word order.

Not all extended testing of informal assessments needs to yield as many measures as the example just described. There are times when it is desirable to compare only one retesting *n* minutes or hours later. Such a simple extension still yields three measures:

1. Original score
2. Ease of learning
   a. number of repetitions
   b. time
   c. feelings
   d. immediate recall
3. Retest score

In any extended testing, it is essential that the teacher look directly, microscopically, and comparatively at the learning process. Just as psychologists did with the early laboratory work on immediate recall, teachers in the classroom can take a close look at the components of learning.

In those instances where the teacher is concerned with comparing learning competency between class members, controls can be set that apply *equally* to each class member in such areas as learning time per symbol, number of repetitions, and/or amount of time to make meaningful applications.

Tests in this diagnostic aid cover both *cognitive areas* (vocabulary, syntax, thinking and comprehension patterns) and *affective areas* (interests and attitudes).

Range of Tests

Grades and/or ages for administering each test in the *Diagnosis File* are included with the data for the test and can also be seen in the "Test Overview Sheet" on pages 4-5. However, it is important to stress that many of the tests are wide-range tests — that is, they can be administered to preschool through high school students. In this manner comparative scores may be plotted and reported over the years. Of some advantage is the fact that all of the tests are under one cover available for duplicating.

Summary Statement

This section covers four areas in the use of the *On-the-Spot Reading Diagnosis File:* survey of test contents, learning styles, extended testing, and range of ability levels tested.

References

Blanton, William, and Terry Bullock, "Cognitive Style and Reading Behavior," *Reading World* (May 1973).

Durrell, Donald. Durrell Analysis of Reading Difficulty. New York: Harcourt Brace Jovanovich, Inc., 1955, 1978.

Glass, Gerald G. *Teaching Decoding as Separate from Reading*. Garden City, N.Y.: Adelphi University Press, 1973.

LaPray, Margaret, and Ramon Ross, "The Graded Word List: Quick Gauge of Reading Ability," *Journal of Reading*. No. 125 (Jan. 1969), 305-07.

Mills, Robert E. Learning Methods Test. Ft. Lauderdale, Fla.: The Mills Center, 1512 E. Broward Blvd., 1955.

SECTION II

assessing visual, auditory, and motor development

(Contains Tests 1 through 5)

Visual, auditory, and motor developmental tests included in this section are designed for use with preschool and primary grade children. However, for students who are not native speakers of English, who are having learning difficulties, or who are diagnosed as dyslexic (unable to read), the tests may be administered at ANY age level.

According to studies, visual and auditory perception measures are better predictors of a young child's ability to learn to read than is an intelligence score. Tests 1, 2, and 4 are included to help the teacher to assess these areas.

Directionality, if well established in the area of letters and words even before the process of reading is begun, will simplify beginning reading. Teachers who copy captions on the preschool child's (nursery, kindergarten) drawings AS the child observes are forming the letters and words in the right sequence and in the correct direction. The early childhood teacher writes on drawings, on charts, on sentence strips, and on the chalkboard IN THE PRESENCE of the children so that directionality is often observed — not because the young child is expected to read at this point, but as a *readiness* for reading. The teacher may even slide a finger from left to right under the titles of books when reading to the children. Test 3 is a test of sequencing and directionality.

Motor development, as measured in Test 5, is of additional interest to the teacher of reading. A few significant correlations have been reported between success in learning to read in grades 1 and 2 and in well-developed motor skills. This correlation becomes less significant from grade 3 on.

The following Test Guide (Table III) includes enough data about the five tests in this section to enable the teacher to tell at a glance which tests are appropriate for his/her particular students.

Table III
Test Guide 1-5

	Test	Title	Ages	Minutes	Appropriate for
D E V E L O P M E N T A L T E S T S	1	Developmental Visual Perception (DVP)	4-8+	5	young beginning readers or older students in difficulty (dyslexic)
	2	Visual Perception Motor Free (VP/MF)	4-8+	3	young beginning readers or older students in difficulty
	3	Visual Sequencing (VS)	5-10+	1	screening slow readers to measure regressions
	4	Auditory Perception (AP) Part I Part II	4-5+ 6-11	5 5	screening beginning readers or older students in difficulty
	5	Motor Development (MD)	5-8+	12	screening to ascertain whether a developmental lag exists

Test 1 DEVELOPMENTAL VISUAL PERCEPTION (DVP)

Description: The Developmental Visual Perception Test (DVP) consists of six figures to be copied by the student. (See page 15.)

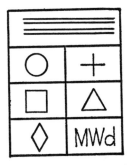

Appropriate for: young students who are beginning the reading process. The DVP is also appropriate for older students who have difficulty in recognizing their own names, or who are learning to read in English as a second language.

Ages: 4-8+, or older students with learning difficulties.

Testing Time: 5 minutes.

Directions for Use:

Administer the DVP individually, as follows:
1. Place a copy of the DVP (page 15) in front of the student in the usual writing position. Observe whether the student rotates the paper and if he does, ask him NOT to do this.
2. Present these oral directions:
    ● "Let's count the number of figures on this paper: 1-2-3-4-5-6."
    ● "Look carefully at the first figure."
    ● "Copy a circle in the space directly below. Do the best you can."

NOTE: For preschool children it is advisable to draw the figures and give them a chance to *imitate* each figure after you have drawn it.

3. As soon as the test sheet is completed, remove it.
4. Place a clean piece of paper in front of the student with directions as follows: "Draw as many of the six figures as you can remember on this paper."

Scoring the Test: While the student is taking the test, watch for signs of difficulty, such as:

- poor line control — shaky or sketchy
- inability to draw distinct angles
- gross lack of closure
- figure rotation of 45° or more ✗ for +

These significant observations, along with an analysis of the Data Sheet, will help you to assess the *quality* of reproduction.

To score the student as passing or failing, use the DVP Data Sheet found immediately before the test (page 14). Most students will be able to pass all of the tests until the first failure, and will fail all figures beyond this point. For these students, scoring is simple: write the "Age Norm" of the highest figure passed.

In cases where the student fails at one level and passes a level beyond, add 1 year for each level passed. For example:

> Student X, aged 7, passes the first 3 figures but fails the 4th figure. However, he passes the 6th, which is the most difficult figure.

	Score
1. Highest level consecutively passed	5-year level
2. Plus 1 year for each level passed beyond this point regardless of number of failures in between	+ 1 year for passing figure 6
DVP Age	6- year level
Chronological Age	7 years

This gives him a deficit of 1 year in developmental visual perception.

When tested on immediate recall, student X remembered only 2 figures, so his performance is scored as inadequate. (See test form.) His test performance behavior in immediate recall is checked as:

confident _____   insecure __✓____

cooperative __✓____   reluctant _____

4 figures or more — adequate _____

3 figures or less — inadequate __✓____

Quality: as expected _____ above _____ below __✓___

The quality is checked as below average because, although he is 7 years old, his circle lacked closure; the + had a slanted vertical, and his square was almost a rectangle.

In interpreting the scores of student X, it seems likely that he was given practice in copying letters before he had learned to cope with closure and angles as required in copying the triangle and diamond.

This test yields the following five measures:
  (1) Observation of behavior
  (2) Comparison of chronological age with developmental visual perception age
  (3) Ability to copy or imitate
  (4) Quality of reproduction
  (5) Immediate memory or recall

Remediation: To provide remedial help for students who do poorly on the DVP, assign tasks similar to those found in the test. For students needing help in forming the figures, use:

> Winterhaven Templates
> Developmental Learning Materials
> Marianne Frostig Visual Motor Training

NOTE: See "References" at the end of this section for a complete listing of source materials, publishers and their addresses.

DVP Data Sheet

(1) Three-year-olds typically start at the bottom of the circle in this manner: For this age group, score as correct those lines that are more circular than angular.

+ Plus if circular   − Minus if angular.

(2) Four-year-olds have very little difficulty with the vertical line, but they have two problems: one with the horizontal, and the other with intersecting the vertical.

(3) Five-year-olds can usually manage parallel lines and are able to reproduce slightly more of a square than a rectangle.

(4) Six-year-olds typically form an identifiable triangle with a slight tilt to the base line.

(5) Seven-year-olds typically elongate the diamond and sometimes make concave lines when doing this.

(6) Eight-year-olds typically copy these 3 letters within the space provided and without reversals.

Test 1 DEVELOPMENTAL VISUAL PERCEPTION (DVP)

Name _____ Grade _____

Date of Test _____ Examiner _____

Observations: _____

_____

_____

Chronological Age _____

yr.   mo.

DVP Age _____

Figure Recall _____

Adequate 4+ _____ _____

Test 2   VISUAL PERCEPTION/MOTOR FREE (VP/MF)

Description: The Visual Perception/Motor Free Test (VP/MF) is made up of figures identical to those on the DVP Test. (See page 18.) The task is one of matching rather than copying. In this test we have a chance to see if the student's problem is one of *visual perception* rather than one of motor coordination.

NOTE: Students who score at or above their chronological age level on the DVP need NOT be given the Visual Perception/ Motor Free Test.

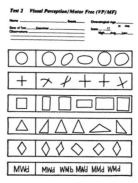

Appropriate for: students at the readiness stage of reading or older students who are experiencing great difficulty in learning to read.

Ages: 4—8+, or older students with learning difficulties.

Testing Time: 3 minutes.

Directions for Use:

Administer the VP/MF individually or in small groups. Directions for presenting the test are as follows:

1. Give the student a copy of the test (page 18).
2. Point to the circle in the box at the top of the left-hand column and direct the student: "See if you can find 2 other circles in this line that look just like the circle in the box."
3. In a similar manner, point to the *plus, square, triangle, diamond,* and *3 letters* and ask the student to find 2 figures just like the one in the box.

Scoring the Test: While the student is taking the test, watch for differences in rate of response between the DVP Test and this test. Also watch for signs of confidence or insecurity.

In scoring the test, each correct figure is worth 1 point. Thus, the total possible score is 12. Students with optimum Visual Perception/Motor Free scores for this test have a performance level typically found in 8-year-olds. Expectation or performance levels for this test are shown in the following chart.

	Below	As Expected	Score	Above CA Expectation
O		3 years old	2	
+		4	4	
□		5	6	
△		6	8	
◇		7	10	
MWd		8	12	

For example:

Student Y has a chronological age of 7 years and 10 months. Since she is closest to her eighth birthday, we will consider her an 8-year-old. She correctly and easily found 2 of each of the figures on the VP/MF. Therefore, she is scored as performing at the *Expected Level.*

Student Y's responses were *rapid* and without any hesitation or changes. Consequently, any deficit in reading demonstrated by Student Y must be the result of factors other than visual perception of form and letters as measured by this test.

Remediation: Students of known average ability or above who score low on the VP/MF — that is, a year or two *below* their chronological age — are in need of remedial exercises.

Low Motor-Free

High DVP Scores: Students who score low on the motor free, but high or above their chronological age on the developmental (Test 1), show strength in kinesthetic involvement, as in copying. These students may demonstrate short attention spans or impulsive responses in matching activities. In this case, use the program called "Try" or puzzles requiring manipulation and attention to form.

Low DVP

High Motor-Free Scores: Students who have high scores or scores above their chronological age on the motor-free test and low scores on the developmental test show lack of fine-muscle coordination. The Getman eye-hand coordination exercises should be helpful with these students.

Test 2   Visual Perception/Motor Free (VP/MF)

Name _____ Grade _____   Chronological Age _____

Date of Test _____ Examiner _____   Score ____ /12   yr.   mo.

Observations: _____

_____   High ____ Avg. ____ Low ____

Test 3   VISUAL SEQUENCING (VS)

Description: The Visual Sequencing Test (VS) is a test of the student's left-to-right orientation. (See page 21). It is also a test of pacing and accuracy of the "return sweep."

Appropriate for: measuring a student's ability to:

- attend to a sequencing task
- scan for detail
- return to the correct line
- avoid regressions
- track letters left to right

The test is also appropriate for students who have overlearned the alphabetical order from *a* through *e*. In cases where this is *not* true, the test can be retyped to include only A B C sequences.

Ages: 5—10+, and older students with learning disabilities.

Testing Time: 1 minute.

Directions for Use:

Administer this test individually or in small groups. Directions for presenting the test are as follows:

1. Give the student a copy of the test (page 21) with these directions: "Draw a line under the letters to connect a b c d e as they appear in that order, but ignore any other letters. DO NOT LIFT your pen from the paper as you rapidly mark from one line to the next." (Use a ballpoint pen.)
2. Demonstrate the following on the chalkboard, being sure to mark the return sweep *rapidly.*

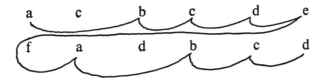

Scoring the Test: While administering this test, continue to watch for signs of confidence such as rapid responses and readiness to continue testing. Conversely, watch for signs of insecurity indicated by taking 4 or more seconds for responses and asking, "Is that right?"

To score the test, use the following point system:

+1 point for every letter in sequence
−1 point for every regression, or incorrect letter marked
−2 points *if* the regression leads to an incorrect letter

The total possible score is 45, that is, 15 for each set of letters.

For example:

Student Z marked these lines as follows:

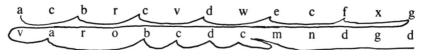

The first line was marked correctly. However, in the second line Student Z regressed to mark an incorrect letter *c*. This incorrect mark means that 2 points will be subtracted from his score.

NOTE: Students with no more than 1 error per 3 lines of letters need no further practice in sequencing.

Remediation: Students who have difficulty completing the VS Test, have several regressions, skip letters, and/or mark letters out of sequence should be given practice in the following types of material:

- Michigan Tracking Booklets
- Developmental Learning Materials
- Visual sequencing teacher-made remedial sheets and similar types of exercises. An example of a teacher-made visual sequencing sheet using a student's name and other words follows:

```
Spell a word.
Mark the letters, as in the first example:
   John        a  l  m  b  J  H  o  n  h  s  i  n
   boy         z  b  x  o  n  y  o  g  u  r  s
   dark        l  n  d  m  a  o  g  r  s  t  u  k
   jump        j  n  m  u  p  m  r  t  l  p  z  x
   skip        q  s  c  k  d  i  e  f  p  b  g  h
   ride        n  r  u  m  i  d  c  b  d  e  l  a
```

NOTE: Time the student daily for a week with similar exercises.

- In some cases it could be helpful to type on a ditto the student's name interspersed with other words at the rate of 3 names per line, as in the following example. (This should be marked in a manner similar to the VS Test.)

```
John jump up or John John can run but
Mary and John or John brother or John
and his friend John John need to beat John
and she can be Ann John for jump John John
John Mary Ann Jack Joe John and her best John
```

Test 3   VISUAL SEQUENCING (VS)

Name _____ Grade _____
Date _____ Examiner _____
Observations _____
_____
_____

Chronological Age _____
Score __/15__   yr.   mo.
        __/15__
        __/15__
TOTAL _____out of 45

Mark the letters **a b c d e** as they appear in order.

a	c	b	r	c	v	d	w	e
v	a	r	o	b	c	b	d	e
a	s	t	b	l	q	c	d	e

_____ out of 15

b	a	d	b	c	h	d	e	d
a	b	c	d	x	e	v	a	t
c	a	b	d	c	d	e	d	b

_____ out of 15

d	c	d	e	a	b	c	d	e
d	a	b	c	d	d	e	d	b
a	c	d	e	d	b	c	d	e

_____ out of 15

Test 4   AUDITORY PERCEPTION (AP)

Description: The Auditory Perception Test (AP) is a two-part assessment. (See pages 27-29).

Part I includes measures of:
1. Auditory Receptive Ability
2. Auditory-Visual Association
3. Auditory Memory

Part II includes measures of:
A. Location of Consonant Clusters
B. Blending (one syllable) (tr-ee)
C. Blending (polysyllables) (scam per ing)
D. Syllable Location
E. Auditory Memory (sentences)

Appropriate for: children ready to begin a formal reading program or older students experiencing difficulty in learning to read.

Ages: Part I — 4-5 yrs. 11 mos.
Part II — 6-11.

Testing Time: Part I — 5 minutes.
Part II — 5 minutes.

Directions for Use:

Directions for administering the two parts of the Auditory Perception Test are presented here in sections corresponding to the sections on the student's copy of the test.

PART I

Give the student a copy of Part I of the test, page 27, then give directions as follows:
1. *Auditory Reception*

Identify the pictures for the child:

mouse	*house*	*louse*
doll	*ball*	*hall*
pig	*wig*	*fig*
coat	*boat*	*goat*

Now direct the child as follows:

"Listen carefully.
  Point to the first 3 pictures.
  Put your finger on the HOUSE.
  Put your finger on the MOUSE."

"Point to the next 3 pictures.
  Put your finger on the DOLL.
  Put your finger on the HALL."

"Look at the next row.
  Put your finger on the PIG.
  Put your finger on the WIG."

"Look at the next row.
  Put your finger on the GOAT.
  Put your finger on the COAT."

Reception Score _____ /8

2. Auditory-Visual Association

Read each set of 3 letters aloud. After each set ask the student to point in turn to *P and E, N and P, B and E,* and *M and L.*

Ex.	P B E
	N O P
	B E P
	N M L

Association Score _____ /6

3. Auditory-Memory

Direct the child as follows: "Listen carefully. As soon as I finish, say the same letters that I said." Read the first line of letters in each box at the rate of 1 per second, and wait for the child's response.

If the first set of letters in each box is correctly read, *do not read* the second set.

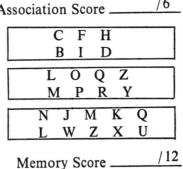

Memory Score _____ /12

PART II

Give the student a copy of Part II of the test, pages 28 and 29, and direct the child as follows:

A. *Location of Consonant Clusters*

Using the first set of boxes, ask the student: "listen and repeat after me: /bl/ as in *blond*. Do you hear the /bl/ at the beginning or end? If it is in the first part of the word put X in the first box; if at the end of the word X the second box. In the second column, put X or X's in whichever box(es) are appropriate." Demonstrate if necessary.

Proceed in the same manner with each of the following consonant clusters, allowing the student to complete each exercise independently.

Ex. ☒☐

/bl/ as in table ☐☐   ☐☐☐ /pl/ as in simpleton

/pl/ as in staple ☐☐   ☐☐☐ /pl/ as in amplify

/pl/ as in plant ☐☐   ☐☐☐ /ch/ as in church

Location Score _____ /6

B. *Blending*

Direct the student: "Listen carefully: *tr ee*. Together the word is *tree*. See if you can do this: *tr ee   tree*." Give the student a chance to blend the example and as much practice as is needed.

Repeat the preceding directions (but do not blend the words) for each of the following words:

bl/oom (bloom)   pl/owed (plowed)

br/oom (broom)   pr/oud (proud)

cl/ash (clash)   dr/ess (dress)

Blending _____ /6

C. *Blending Polysyllabic Words*

Point out the sample polysyllabic word "scampering" to the student. Read this word in syllables, then together as one word; then ask the student to do the same—and make sure this direction is understood.

Now direct the student to read the following four sets of syllables, then to blend each combination together as one word.

re turn ing   returning
es tab blish   establish
un de ci ded   undecided
pro tec tor ate   protectorate

NOTE: Score 1 point for each correctly pronounced syllable *only* when correctly blended in a word or nonword. Example: retai*ning* = 2 points.

Blending _____ /18

D. *Syllable Sound Location*

Complete the first three examples with the student. Read the syllable, then the three sample words. Ask the student to "mark an X where you hear the syllable."

Ex.

/per/*

re*pair*	☐☐
*par*ent	☐☐
com*par*ing	☐☐☐

Present the next two sets in a similar manner.

Mark an X where you hear

/plej/

*play*ful	1 ☐☐	____	____	
re*play*	2 ☐☐	____	____	
com*plac*ent	3 ☐☐☐	____	____	

Mark an X where you hear

/men/

*men*tor	4 ☐☐	____	____	
wo*men*	5 ☐☐	____	____	
*men*tioning	6 ☐☐☐	____	____	

Syllables ____ /6

E. *Auditory Memory*

Direct the student to "listen carefully. Repeat these sentences after me." The student needs to pass 1 sentence in each set. If the first sentence in a set is passed, *do not read* the second sentence.

I can swim.
He can dive.

We got up early.
They stayed out late.

It rained during the picnic.
Storm clouds were above us.

Memory ____ /6

---

*This is Hockett's notation. See Charles Hockett, *A Course in Modern Linguistics* (New York: Macmillan, 1958).

Scoring the Test: Following are typical scores for both parts of the AP Test.

Part 1 has 26 points.

Typical scores are:

4 years old	18—21
5 years old	22—24
5 years 11 mo.	25—26

Part II has 42 points.

Typical scores for Parts I and II combined:

6 years old	40—45
7 years old	46—50
8 years old	51—55
9 years old	56—60
10 years old	61 and up

Of first interest is the *total* score showing how the student compares with others in his age group. However, of even greater importance and value are the student's *areas of strengths* (those subtests on which he makes NO errors) and his *areas of need* (those subtests on which he scores 75% or less). For example:

Student A, age 9, had a total score of 58, which is within the expected range for his age. His scores were perfect on Part I and all but one subtest on Part II. On subtest E, Auditory Memory, he was unable to repeat any sentences on an immediate recall basis.

Remediation: Scores on each subtest need to be carefully analyzed, and those scores of 75% or less should lead to exercises directly patterned after the items in the test.

In the case of Student A, above, dictate simple sentences to be listened to and repeated.

Test 4 | AUDITORY PERCEPTION (AP)

Name _____ Grade _____ Chronological Age _____

                                                              yr.   mo.

Date of Test _____ Examiner _____
Observations: _____
_____   Part I _____ /26
_____   Part II _____ /68

PART I

1. Auditory Reception

1 ___/___

2 ___/___

3 ___/___

4 ___/___

Reception Score _____ /8

2. Auditory-Visual Association

Ex.	
	P B E
	N O P
	B E P
	N M L

Association Score _____ /6

3. Auditory Memory

C F H
B I D

L O Q Z
M P R Y

N J M K Q
L W Z X U

Auditory Score _____ / 12

Test 4   AP (cont.)

A. Location of Consonant Clusters

Ex.

Location Score _____ /6

B. Blending

1_____   4_____

2_____   5_____

3_____   6_____

Blending Score _____ /6

Test 4   AP (cont.)

C. Blending Polysyllabic Words:

      Ex. *scam per ing*
           scampering

      1. _____

      2. _____

      3. _____

      4. _____

Blending ___/18___

D. Syllable-Sound Location

      Ex.

  1 □□
  2 □□
  3 □□□
  4 □□
  5 □□
  6 □□□

Syllables ___/6___

E. Auditory Memory

_____ _____ _____

_____ _____ _____ _____

_____ _____ _____ _____ _____

1 point for a correct 3-word sentence
2 points for a correct 4-word sentence
3 points for a correct 5-word sentence
(No partial scores)

Memory ___/6___

Test 5   MOTOR DEVELOPMENT TEST (MD)

Description: The Motor Development Test (MD) includes some measurement of the child's dominance, gross coordination, fine coordination, and skill in coding. (See pages 33-35.)

Appropriate for: children who tested low on Development Visual Preparation Test (DVP), who appear uncoordinated, and/or are reading disabled.

Ages: 5—8, or older children with learning disabilities.

Testing Time: approximately 12 minutes.

Directions for Use:
Administer the Motor Development Test individually, reading directions to the student directly from the test pages (33-35).
To prepare for the test, you will need to assemble the following materials:
- 1 crumpled sheet of typing paper, round in shape
- 6″ square of cardboard with a pinhole in the center
- 1 toilet-roll tube
- 1 straight chalk-line, 6′ long, on the floor
- 1 jump rope
- an X on the chalkboard
- 2 test sheets

Scoring the Test:

Observations: In establishing dominance there are two trials in each sphere. However, if the student alternates with left and right, it may be necessary to add a third trial in order to establish dominance.

Children who catch equally well with their left and right hands, or who can write with either hand, are classed as ambidextrous. This segment of our population is a very small percent, and learning problems are NOT particularly associated with this group.

Dominantly left-handed children who have changed to right-handedness may show signs of tension, even to the point of stuttering. Learning disability specialists are in agreement that a switch of this kind is inadvisable.

NOTE: Mixed dominance is a measurement of interest to us, but according to present research *not* as yet significantly related to remedial reading problems.

Scoring: The first part of the MD has no total raw score. The test gives basically the following information:

Dominance Table of Seven Cases

Case #	Eyed	Handed	Footed	Dominance
1	Lt	Rt	Lt	Mixed
2	Rt	Lt	Rt	Mixed
3	Rt	Rt	Lt	Mixed
4	Lt	Lt	Rt	Mixed
5	Rt/Lt	Rt/Lt		Ambidextrous
6	Rt	Rt	Rt	Rt Dominant
7	Lt	Lt	Lt	Lt Dominant

The language areas of visual perception for reading and handedness for writing are controlled by the broca area in the left side of the brain. Cases 1 and 2 above have mixed dominance in language areas, therefore some authorities feel that they would be likely to have reading difficulties. However, other experts such as Albert Harris disagree with this theory. Because there is evidence on both sides, it would be advisable to watch such cases with a special interest.

Empirically, cases 4 and 7 are instances of students who are left in eyedness and handedness, and most of these students function as expected in reading.

Gross coordination is a part of the total data on remedial reading cases. This is an additional measure of the student's physical maturity. *Fine motor coordination* is another measure of physical maturity. In addition, skill in fine motor coordination correlates with such tasks as writing and reading.

Results of coding tasks, the second part of the MD, are of particular interest to remedial reading teachers since there is a significant correlation between effectiveness in reading and coding. For example:

Student B is 7 years old. He has mixed dominance, being left-eyed and right-handed. There is a possibility that he is actually left-handed and was changed by his parents. His record shows immature speech through Grade 1.

His gross coordination appears more like that of a 6-year-old. His skip is an alternating hop more than a skip, and he is unable to jump rope.

His coding score is 30, which places him at the 6-year-old level, or with a deficit score of 1 year.

Student B CA 7-0		Page	
Dominance	*Mixed* (with complications)	33	Dominance
Gross Coordination	6-0	34	Gross Coordination
Fine Coordination	6-0	34	Fine Coordination

Remediation: In general, scoring the MD Test is a matter of comparing the student's chronological age with tasks typically achieved by students at the same age, above, or below that age. In cases of normal intelligence where a deficit appears, work should be done on tasks similar to those in the test.

Student B, in the case example above, needs to be permitted to use his dominant or left hand. This change alone may improve his gross and fine muscle coordination. However, a strong physical education program will certainly help his gross motor coordination. Special attention should be given to demonstrations and practice in skipping forward and in place, and also in jumping rope.

In addition, student B needs practice with all kinds of numbers, letters, and position codes. Here is an example of a position code.

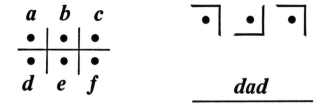

dad

Test 5 MOTOR DEVELOPMENT TEST (MD)

Name _____ Grade _____ Chronological Age _____

                                                                             yr.   mo.

Date of Test _____ Examiner _____   Dominance _____

Observations: _____   Gross Coordination _____

_____   Fine Coordination _____

_____

Material: One crumpled-up sheet of typing paper.

Handedness

Directions: "Try to catch this wad of paper. Whether you catch it or not is unimportant. I want to see how *CLOSE* you come to catching it, using one hand only."

	Right	Left	Observations
Catch with 1 hand			
2 throws to center body			
2 throws to right of body			
2 throws to left of body			

                                               _____right   _____left

Footedness

Directions: "Try to kick this wad of paper. Whether you kick it or not is unimportant. I want to see how *CLOSE* you come to kicking it."

	Right	Left	Observations
2 throws to center space			
2 throws to right foot			
2 throws to left foot			

                                               _____right   _____left

Eyedness

Directions:

"Look through the pinhole at this X" (5' away).

Tube focus: "Look at the X" (5' away).

	Right	Left	Observations

                                               _____ right   _____left

Dominance: Right _____

              Left _____

              Mixed _____

    Ambidextrous _____

Test 5 MD (cont.)

Gross Coordination

Directions:

"Walk backwards 6′ toe to heel."
"Skip around the room once."
"Jump 10 times."
(Demonstrate.)
"Skip rope 10 times."
   (Demonstrate.)

Age	Observations
5	
6	
7	
7	

Gross Coordination Age_____

Fine Coordination

Directions:

"Try to make 'spider fingers.'"
   (Demonstrate as directed
   below.*) "Touch thumb and
   fingers eight times."
"Write your name (from memory)."
Coding (see below).

Age	
5	_____
6	
7	35-40
8	41-45

*Step 1: Press the right thumb print to the left index finger print. Step 2: Next reach up and

connect the right index print to the left thumb print. Step 3: Release step 1. Pivot fingers upward and repeat step 2.

Test 5 MD (cont.)

Coding

Directions: "Look carefully at the 5 figures below. Each figure has a mark inside it." Give the student about 10 seconds to study the marks, then say, "I want these marks put inside the blank figures below."

Next, point to the box set apart for practice, Give the student a chance to mark this. Be sure that the marks are correct. As soon as the practice exercise is correctly completed, say, "Begin by marking each figure in turn without skipping any. Go right on to the next line and keep on working until I ask you to stop. Start now." Allow the student 2 minutes.

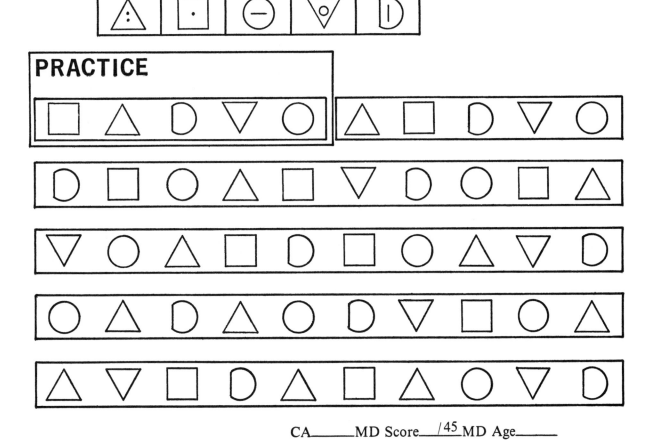

CA_____MD Score__/45__MD Age_____

Test 5
MOTOR DEVELOPMENTAL LEVEL

Scoring Table	
Typical Age	Score Range
5	15-24
6	25-34
7	35-40
8	41-45

Section II Summary

The five tests in Section II yield the following measures:

Test	Title	Measures
1	Developmental Visual Perception (DVP)	Ability to visually perceive and copy geometric forms and letters
2	Visual Perception/Motor Free (VP/MF)	Ability to match figures as compared with ability to copy figures identical to those in Test 1
3	Visual Sequencing (VS)	Ability to track rapidly, accurately, and in the right direction
4	Auditory Perception (AP)	Auditory receptiveness visual/auditory association Memory Consonant clusters Syllable sound location Sentence memory
5	Motor Development (MD)	Gross motor ability Fine motor coordination Coding skill

All of these skills and abilities are of interest to reading instructors, and most of them can be taught if they are not yet developed to the student's potential.

References

Bender, Lauretta. *A Visual Gestalt Test and Its Clinical Use.* (Research Monograph, No. 3.) New York: American Orthopsychiatric Association, 1938.

Berry, Keith E., and Norman A. Buktenica. Developmental Test of Visual-Motor Integration. Chicago: Follett, 1967.

Benton, Arthur L. The Revised Visual Retention Test. New York: Psychological Corporation, 1963.

Cheves, Ruth, *Face and Figure Puzzles.* Boston: New York Times Teaching Resources.

Colarusso, Ronald P., and Donald D. Hammil. Motor-Free Visual Perception Test. San Rafael, Ca.: Academic Therapy Publications, 1972.

Fernald, Grace M. *Remedial Techniques in Basic School Subjects.* New York: McGraw-Hill, 1943.

Frostig, Marianne, and D. Horne. *The Frostig Program for the Development of Visual Perception.* Chicago: Follett, 1964.

Geake, Robert R., and Donald E. P. Smith. *Visual Tracking.* (Michigan Tracking Program.) Ann Arbor: Ann Arbor Publishers, 1962.

Getman, Gerald N. "The Visuomotor Complex in the Acquisition of Learning Skills," in Jerome Hellmuch (ed.), *Learning Disorders,* Vol. 1. Seattle: Special Child Publications, 1965.

Hatton, Daniel A., Frank J. Pizzzat, and Jerome Pelkowski. *Perceptual Bingo.* Boston: New York Times Teaching Resources.

Hockett, Charles. *A Course in Modern Linguistics.* New York: Macmillan, 1958.

Kelly, J.C. *Clinician's Handbook for Auditory Training.* Washington, D.C.: Alexander Graham Bell Associates for the Deaf, Inc., 1973.

Kirk, Samuel, and Winifred D. Kirk. *Psycholinguistic Learning Disabilities: Diagnosis and Remediation.* Urbana, Ill.: University of Illinois Press, 1971.

Koppitz, Elizabeth M. The Bender-Gestalt Test for Young Children. New York: Grune and Stratton, 1964.

Lindamood, Charles, and Patricia Lindamood. *Auditory Discrimination in Depth.* Boston: New York Times Teaching Resources, 1975.

Roach, Eugene G., and Newell C. Kephart. The Purdue Perceptual-Motor Survey. Columbus, Ohio: Merrill, 1966.

Sloan, William. The Lincoln-Oseretsky Motor Development Scale. Chicago: Stoelting Co., 1956.

Slosson, Richard L. Slosson Drawing Coordination Test for Children and Adults. East Aurora, N.Y.: Slosson Educational Publications, Inc., 1967.

"Try." New York: Noble & Noble, Inc., 245 E. 47th Street, N.Y. 10017.

Visual Sequential Memory Exercises. Niles, Ill.: Developmental Learning Materials, 1972.

Wechsler, David. *Wechsler Intelligence Scale for Children,* Revised. New York: Psychological Corporation, 1974.

Winter Haven Lions Research Foundation, Inc., Box 112, Winter Haven, Fla. 33880.

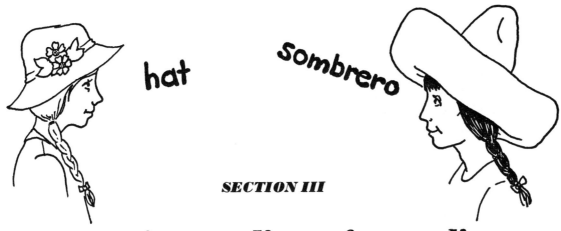

SECTION III

assessing readiness for reading

(Contains Tests 6 through 10)

Scores from prereading tests measure the child's readiness for formal reading instruction. Assessment devices included in this section deal with reading readiness, intellectual capacity, and English/Spanish language dominance.

In our language the direction of the letters of the alphabet is crucial to correct identification. Most letters are sources of horizontal confusion. In fact, there are only six lower case letters that cannot be reversed horizontally: *i o v w x*; and at least two of these letters are seldom seen by a beginning reader: *v, x*. Therefore, it is not surprising that children who are learning to read and write have a high instance of reversals. This condition is not a cause for panic. Parents can be helped to appreciate the commonness of reversals in grades 1 and 2, and can be helped to understand that usually by grade 3 the letter directions are well established. Test 6 is included to alert both the parent and the teacher to the high instances of reversals and to monitor the student's improvement in this area.

Reading readiness tests serve as predictors of success in beginning reading insofar as they have subskills identical to those found in beginning reading. Subskills such as visual discrimination of letters, words, and sentences, and auditory discrimination of initial consonant sounds are examples of such subskills that are included in Test 7.

Even though we recognize that intelligence measures do not correlate significantly with success in beginning reading, there are features of intelligence of special concern to us. One is an assessment of present achievement; another is an awareness of detail; and finally, a measure of vocabulary knowledge. Test 8 measures awareness of detail. Test 9 measures awareness of details and vocabulary knowledge. Both of these measures are assessments of capacity to learn, but more directly they are measures of the child's exposure to types of information which we consider part of the child's common heritage.

Both Tests 7 and 8 can be used as extended testing techniques, particularly in instances where students score below their expected age level. Immediately following the test, show the student the items missed, and retest at a later time. As explained in Section I, this gives you three sets of scores:

1. Original score
2. Observations of Learning Time, etc.
3. Retest score

In English/Spanish-speaking areas students run the gamut from English dominant, Spanish dominant, bilingual, to confused or non-fluent in either language. Obviously these four basic ability levels will not respond equally well to a single-track program. However, before decisions are made on the types of programs to fit populations like this, some assessment of language dominance should be given. Test 10 is designed for this purpose.

The following Test Guide (Table IV) presents a brief overview of the five tests in this section.

Table IV
Test Guide 6-10

	Test	Title	Ages	Minutes	Appropriate for:
R E A D I N E S S	6	Reversal Letters and Words (RLW)	5-9+	10	screening beginning readers to assess the extent of reversals
	7	Personalized Reading Readiness (PRR)	5-6+	10	assessing children's readiness to begin reading
I N T E L L I G E N C E	8	Nonverbal Intelligence (NI)	4-8+	5	assessing the capacity of children to note detail
	9	Body/Receptive Vocabulary (BRV)	4-6 / 7-12	2 / 5	assessing children's capacity
E S L	10	Language Dominance English/Spanish (LD E/S) Part I / Part II	to 4½-6 + / 6-11	5	primarily for screening young Mexican-American, Puerto Rican, or Spanish children of unknown language dominance

Test 6   REVERSAL LETTERS AND WORDS (RLW)

Description: This test consists of three tasks appropriate for use with young children before they are able to read:

> Task 1. Find letters in the same direction.
> Task 2. Find words in the same direction.
> Task 3. Find letters turned in the correct direction.

Tasks 4 and 5 are for students able to read, and are measures of the student's ability to recognize words in the same direction.

Appropriate for: children who experience difficulty in beginning reading, or older students with a persistent reversal problem.

Ages: 5—9+, or older students with learning disabilities

Testing Time: 10 minutes.

Directions for Use:

Administer this test, on pages 44-45, individually, reading the following directions for the five subtests included:

1. "Choose the bottom letters that are just like the top letters and in the same direction."
2. "Point to the ones that are the same, and turned in the same direction."
3. "Point to the words that are written correctly to match the picture."
4. "Point to the words written in the correct direction."
5. "Read aloud."

Scoring the Test: Allow one point for each correct answer. The optimum score possible is 38. However, our concern is whether the student needs help at the matching level or with letters and words in isolation. Subtests 1 and 2 are at the matching level. Subtests 3 and 4 show letters and words in isolation, and involve a more difficult task than matching.

Subtest 5, since it requires the student to read the underlined words, is the most difficult task of all. Words NOT underlined may be read by the teacher IF necessary.

In general, each student should be checked as passing or failing each subtest. The following table can be used for this purpose.

PASSING RAW SCORES

Chronological Ages CA	Subtest	1	2	3	4	5
5 yrs. old		5+	5+	5+		
6 yrs. old		6	6	6	7	4
7 yrs. old		7	7	7	8	4
8 yrs. old		8	8	8	9	5
9 yrs. old		8	8	8	10	6

(5+ means 5 and up)

For example, consider the performance of Student C:

5 yrs. old	6 OK	6 OK	4 Failed

Student C, who has a chronological age of 5, scored 6 out of 10 on subtest 1. This means that she easily passed the subtest. On subtest 2 she scored 6 out of 8 and passed easily. On subtest 3 she scored 4 out of 8, which is one point below passing.

Remediation: In the case of Student C, she is comfortable and accurate at the matching state. She needs instruction in identifying letters in isolation. One program designed to introduce letters in more than one position is the *A B C and Me Book* listed in the "References" at the end of this section. Outstanding A B C books such as those by Brian Wildsmith, Don Crewe, and Dr. Seuss are useful, too.

In general, students who test below the passing score in the RLW have a poor or incorrectly learned sense of direction. For these students, daily modeling on a one-to-one basis is needed to establish the correct direction. Immediate and supervised copying by the student helps to establish new patterns.

Preventing bad habits is our goal. To prevent any incorrect practice on letters and words, remember to model them in a controlled *introduction,* that is, form the letters as the child watches.

To extinguish an incorrect response and to have to reteach directionality is far more difficult than to introduce it with built-in monitored safety measures.

The following are several suggested techniques:

1. Use a variation of Fernald so that the child traces and says the word as he or she traces it.
2. Trace letters individually on the child's back to improve the ability to *feel* letter forms.
   Give the child exercises similar to those in the test to provide *practice* in identifying similarities.
4. Have students observe as the teacher WRITES the new words being presented in the left-to-right direction rather than presenting words on flashcards which allow the students to zero in on an end, a medial letter and an incorrect direction.

It is also suggested that you try extended testing (ET). Help the child to discover ALL of the correct answers. Twenty minutes later readminister the test and compare the score with the original.

Test 6 REVERSAL LETTERS AND WORDS (RLW)

Name _____ Grade _____ Chronological Age _____

yr.   mo.

Date of Test _____ Examiner _____

Observations: _____ Score _____ /40

_____

5-year-olds _____ /24

ET

Letters — Same or Different	/8	_____
Word — Same or Different	/8	_____
Letter Directionality	/8	_____
Word Directionality	/10	_____
Words in Context	/6	_____

Ages 5-9

1.

A	B	C	D	E	F	G	H	I	J	K	L
Ɐ	ꓭ	C	D	E	Ⅎ	G	H	I	ꞁ	K	L

Score ____ /8 ET _____

2.

MOM	go	no	Me
WOM	go	on	Me

we	not	net	top
we	ton	net	pot

see	from	proud	saw
sea	for	proud	was

dig	want	cop	but
pig	want	cop	but

Score ____ /8 ET _____

3.

A	ꓭ	C	D	Ǝ	F	Ɠ	H	ꞁ	L	K	ꓕ	M

Score ____ /8 ET _____

Test 6   RLW (cont.)

Ages 6-9

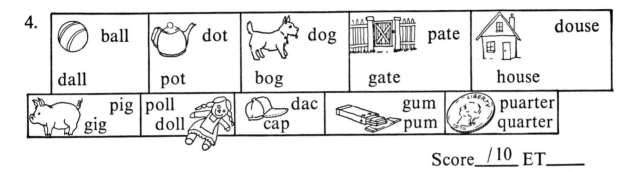

4.

ball	dot	dog	pate	douse
dall	pot	bog	gate	house

pig	poll	dac	gum	puarter
gig	doll	cap	pum	quarter

Score ___/10___ ET_____

5.

No I was not on the slide.
I saw you take a bad fall.
You fell like a ton of bricks.

Score ___/6___ ET_____

Test 7   PERSONALIZED READING READINESS (PRR)

Description: This is a test of a number of important prereading skills. It is divided into seven parts, measuring one of the following skills: letter identification, word matching, matching upper and lower case letters, matching sounds to pictures, identifying name, matching sentences, and distinguishing between alike and different initial sounds. (See pages 48-49.)

Appropriate for: students who have not yet begun reading and who are in kindergarten or grade 1, or for students who are experiencing difficulty in beginning reading regardless of age.

Ages: 5—6+, or older students who have reading disabilities.

Testing Time: 10 minutes.

Directions for Use:
Prepare a personalized copy of the test (pages 48-49) with a few students' names typed on several of the blank lines in part 5. Be sure to include the name of the student being tested. Then administer the seven subtests included as follows:

1. Letter Identification
   Direct the child: "Look at the large box at the top of the page. Circle all of the letters in your *first* name."
   NOTE: Establish that the child knows his/her first name.

2. Word Matching
   Note that the child does *not* need to be able to read any of the words in this subtest, only to *match* them. Direct the child: "Look at the small bicycle below with the word beside it. In the square below the picture of a bicycle, can you find the same set of letters as the word written in small type? Circle the word."
   Repeat similar directions for *sun, ball and bat,* and *cat.*

3. Matching Upper and Lower Case Letters
   Direct the student as follows: "See the top row of capital letters? On the second row are the same letters written in lower case. Notice the capital *B* has a dotted line to the lower case *b.* Go over this line with your pencil. Now connect each of the other capital letters with the lower case letter that matches it."

4. Matching Initial Sounds to Pictures
   Direct the student: "Point to the pictures and say the words after me — *balloon, candy cane, house, moon,* and *sun.* Now listen carefully. Point to the picture that sounds like the beginning of *cat.*" (Help the child to find the candy cane, if necessary.)
   Continue with *sad, mom, ball,* and *happy.*

5. Identifying Name (from among others)

Direct the student: "Look at all of the names in the box. Can you find and circle your name?"

NOTE: The student's name should have been typed on one of the blank lines.

6. Matching Sentences

Direct the student: "Look at the small printed sentence. Can you find a sentence in the box below with the same words in it? Circle the sentence. Do the same for the next small sentence."

7. Initial Sounds Alike or Different

Direct the student as follows: "Say the words in the pictures *after* me — *teapot-tent, scissors-sailboat, fish-waves, boat-ring, kitten-kite, dog-ball, house-horse,* and *moon-mop.* Now go back to the *teapot-tent.* Do these words begin alike? If they sound alike, put a + in the square. If they sound different, do not put any mark at all. See if you can complete the other pictures by yourself."

Scoring the Test: Scoring for the seven parts of the test is as follows:

1. Letter Identification (First Name)
   /6 optimum for total name (Al or Jennifer)
   /3 for 1/2 right (A as 1/2 of *Al* or Jenn as 1/2 of Jennifer, unless Jenn is a nickname in which case *full* credit should be given)
   Less than 1/2 gets *no* score.
2. Word Matching
   /4 optimum
3. Matching Upper and Lower Case Letters
   /5 optimum
4. Matching Initial Sounds to Pictures
   /5 optimum
5. Identifying Name (from among others)
   /6 optimum
6. Matching Sentences
   /7 optimum
7. Initial Sounds Alike or Different
   /5 optimum

Total Score: 38   34-38   Superior
                    30-33   Good
                    29 or less   Questionable

Students with scores of 34 to 38 should be able to enter a formal reading program without difficulty.

Students with scores of 30 to 34 have a good prognosis. However, if all 5 of the points were missed on subtest 7, the student obviously needs help with initial sounds.

Students with scores of 29 or less need more instruction in prereading; that is, they need practice in exercises similar to those found in this test.

Test 7 PERSONALIZED READING READINESS (PRR)

Name _____ Grade _____   Chronological Age _____
                                                              yr.   mo.
Date of Test _____ Examiner _____   Raw Score _____
Observations: _____   superior _____
_____   good _____
_____   questionable _____

1. Letter Identification

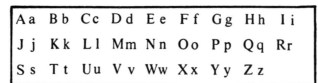

```
Aa  Bb  Cc  Dd  Ee  Ff  Gg  Hh  Ii
Jj  Kk  Ll  Mm  Nn  Oo  Pp  Qq  Rr
Ss  Tt  Uu  Vv  Ww  Xx  Yy  Zz
```

2. Word Matching

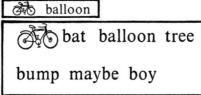

balloon — bat balloon tree bump maybe boy

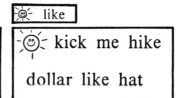

like — kick me hike dollar like hat

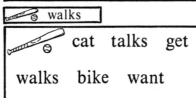

walks — cat talks get walks bike want

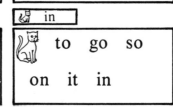

in — to go so on it in

3. Matching Upper and Lower Case Letters

B   C   A   W   G   P

a   b   c   p   g   w

4. Matching Sounds to Pictures

Test 7 PRR (cont.)

5. Identifying Name

Mary	Pam	Vickie
John	Ann	Lynn
Ray	Jim	————
	————	————	————
————	————	————

6. Matching Sentences

See the big ball.

See the little ball.

See the big ball.

See the balloon.

See the ball.

See the balloon.

Sew the balloon.

7. Initial Sounds — Alike or Different

Test 8   NON-VERBAL INTELLIGENCE (NI)

Description: The Non-Verbal Intelligence Test (NI) measures children's observation of details in a familiar object — their own faces. (See page 53.)

Appropriate for: children for whom a mental measurement is needed.

Ages: 4—8+, or older children with language problems.

Testing Time: 5 minutes.

Directions for Use:
Administer the NI individually or in small groups as follows:
1. Place a mirror in a position so that the child's face can be easily seen even when he or she is seated. Give the child a copy of the test (page 53).
2. Say, "Look at your face in the mirror. Draw everything you see. Use this to start your drawing." (Point to the large egg-head on the paper.)
3. Give the child a No. 2 pencil with no eraser.

Scoring the Test: See the "NI Scoring Examples" on page 52 for detailed scoring instructions. The last TOTAL PROPORTIONS of 2 points is allowed if the student already has 15 points and draws in these proportions:

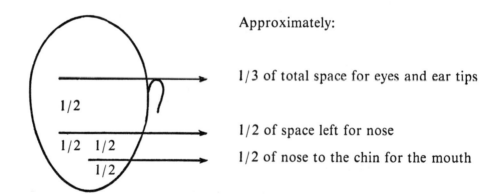

Approximately:

1/3 of total space for eyes and ear tips

1/2 of space left for nose

1/2 of nose to the chin for the mouth

For example: Student E comes from a migrant family and although his chronological age is 6, his egghead drawing looks like that of a 4-year-old. If the test was given after only a few days at school, chances are he has never held a pencil or crayon before. It would be necessary to give him experience in handling pencils and crayons before making any assessments about his ability to observe detail and his mental alertness.

Conversely, an artistic child, as the result of direct instruction and practice, may rate higher on this measurement than on a verbal-receptive vocabulary test such as Test 9.

Remediation: Students who score low on this test should be given instruction in observation of common forms such as circles, squares, rectangles, and triangles. They should be encouraged to look for these shapes in nature, and to copy these forms on paper.

Our old ideas of intelligence as an unalterable birthright have been replaced by the more hopeful view of intelligence as a measure to be taken in order to build up areas of weakness. Mary Meeker explains this positive view of intelligence in a reference cited at the end of this section.

NI Scoring Examples

4 year old

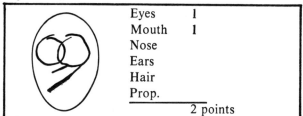

Eyes	1	
Mouth	1	
Nose		
Ears		
Hair		
Prop.		
	2 points	

5 year old

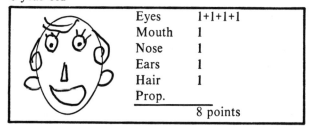

Eyes	1+1	
Mouth	1	
Nose	1	
Ears		
Hair	1	
Prop.		
	5 points	

6 year old

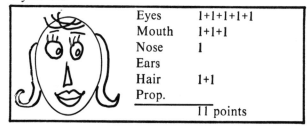

Eyes	1+1+1+1	
Mouth	1	
Nose	1	
Ears	1	
Hair	1	
Prop.		
	8 points	

7 year old

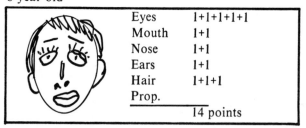

Eyes	1+1+1+1+1	
Mouth	1+1+1	
Nose	1	
Ears		
Hair	1+1	
Prop.		
	11 points	

8 year old

Eyes	1+1+1+1+1	
Mouth	1+1	
Nose	1+1	
Ears	1+1	
Hair	1+1+1	
Prop.		
	14 points	

Expected Scores	Ages
2-4 4	
5-7 5	
8-10 6	
11-13 7	
14-16 8	

Eyes					
Mouth					
Nose					
Hair					
Ears					
Propor.					

SCORING   HIGHEST POSSIBLE 18

EYES	any indication	1
	pupils	1
	lashes	1
	brow	1
	spaced apart (allowed only if eyes already have 2 points)	1
MOUTH	any indication	1
	2 lips	1
	spaced on face (allowed only if lips already have 2 points)	1
NOSE	any indication	1
	nostrils	1
	spaced on face (allowed only if nose already has 2 points)	1
HAIR	any indication	1
	details, waves or styled	1
	spaced on head (allowed only if hair already has 2 points)	1
EARS	any indication	1
	spaced on head at eye level	1
TOTAL PROPORTIONS (only scored after 15+ points)		2

1/3 eyes/ears   1/2 nose   1/2 mouth

Test 8   NON-VERBAL INTELLIGENCE (NI)

Name _____ Grade _____ _____   Chronological Age _____
                                                                              yr.   mo.
Date of Test _____ Examiner _____   Expected Score _____
Observations: _____   Actual Score _____
_____   Comments _____
_____

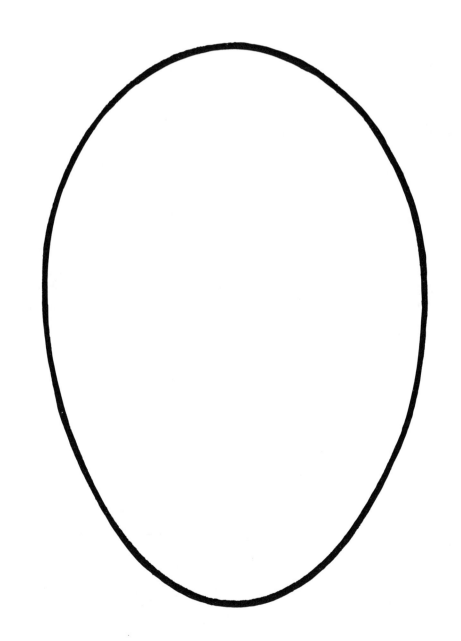

Test 9   BODY/RECEPTIVE VOCABULARY (BRV)

Description: The BRV consists of 48 body parts that are named by the examiner and pointed to by the student. (See page 56.) It is a measure of the student's awareness of body parts.

Appropriate for: children for whom a mental measurement is needed.

Ages: 4-12.

Testing Time: 2 minutes for ages 4-6.
                 5 minutes for ages 7-12.

Directions for Use:
  Administer this test individually, as follows:
1. Give items 1-48 on the test (page 56) to the student orally by having the student point to the parts named. ("Point to your eyes . . . nose . . . mouth . . .")
2. Stop testing at the level in which the student misses 4 out of 6 consecutive responses.

Scoring the Test: In most instances the student will be able to point to the body part as directed. In a few cases, however, this may be ambiguous. For example, when asked to point to his/her skeleton, the student may say, "I can't." In cases such as this, ask the student to tell what the skeleton is made up of.

  Students should be given credit for all items below any six consecutive correct responses.

  For example, Student F is 10 years old. Testing was begun with item 15, and he got six correct responses through item 20. This gives him a base score of 20. He gets credit for all items up to this point.

  He then misses items 22, 26, 28, 29, 30. Testing should stop at item 30 since at this point he has missed 4 out of 6 consecutive items.

$$\text{Base Score} \quad \underset{\underset{25}{+5}}{\underline{20}} \quad + \quad \underset{1}{21} \quad X \quad \underset{1}{23,} \quad \underset{1}{24,} \quad \underset{1}{25} \quad X \quad \underset{1}{27} \quad X \quad X \quad X$$

  As shown in the chart that follows, a score of 25 is more typically found among 8-year-olds than 10-year-olds. Thus, on this one test of verbal receptive body vocabulary, Student F has a two-year deficit.

BRV Typical Scores

Ages		Expected Scores
4	. . . .	2-4
5	. . . .	5-7
5-6 mo	. . . .	8-10
6	. . . .	11-13
6-6 mo	. . . .	14-16

```
7       ...................... 17-19
7-6 mo...................... 20-22
8       ...................... 23-25
8-6 mo...................... 26-28
9       ...................... 29-33
10      ...................... 34-37
11      ...................... 38-41
12      ...................... 42-45
```

Remediation: For a low score in this mental capacity test structure a learning unit to teach body parts. Such a health unit should cover bones, muscles, and internal organs at an appropriate level for the student.

Extended testing (ET) is appropriate for Student F in the example previously presented. Immediately after completing this test, correct any items the student missed and "tell" him the items he did not attempt — at least up to the expected score level for his age. Tell him that you will retest him the following morning. As explained before, you will have three measures of behavior and performance in place of one.

Test 9   *BODY/RECEPTIVE VOCABULARY (BRV)*

Name _____ Grade _____   Chronological Age _____

                                                         yr.   mo.

Date of Test _____ Examiner _____   Raw Score _____ ET _____

Observations _____   Within expected range _____

_____   Above expected range _____

_____   Below expected range _____

"Point to your _____"

Begin here at ages

4,5 .... 6,7 .... 8,9 .... 10+

1 eyes	5 chin	9 feet	13 ankles
2 nose	6 hands	10 waist	14 cheeks
3 mouth	7 legs	11 neck	15 fingers
4 ears	8 arms	12 stomach	16 toes
17 forehead	21 elbow	25 ribs	29 middle finger
18 teeth	22 collar bone	26 shin	30 shoulder blades
19 thumb	23 knee caps	27 finger nails	31 instep
20 eyebrows	24 wrist	28 index finger	32 tongue
33 palms	37 thigh	41 shoulder	45 temples
34 spinal column	38 biceps	42 skelcton	46 hip
35 rib cage	39 ear lobe	43 skull	47 abdomen
36 chest	40 heart	44 tonsils	48 diaphragm

Test 10 LANGUAGE DOMINANCE, English/Spanish (LD E/S)

Description: This test consists of two parts. Part I is designed for preschool and young children, and Part II for older children. Part I includes 8 questions or directions to be responded to by the student (page 60) followed by a letter identification task. Part II includes 36 cards with pictures to be identified by the student either in Spanish or in English. The cards are organized into six levels and are presented in Appendix I (pages 243-245) for easy reproduction and assembly.

Appropriate for: students of undetermined language dominance throughout the elementary grades.

Ages: Part I — 4 to 6 years (for young children only).
Part II — 6-1 to 11 years.

Testing Time: Part I — 5 minutes.
Part II — 2 minutes or more, depending on the student's ability.

Directions for Use: The LD E/S should be administered individually by a *bilingual* instructor and testing should begin with Part I for preschool age children to age 7. Children of 6 and 7 years should begin with the letter identification task. Children 8 or older should begin with the cards.
Following are directions for presenting the two parts of the test.

PART I (4 to 6 Years)

1. Read from the sentences 1 through 8 as they are written in Part I (page 60): odd-numbered questions in English and even-numbered questions in Spanish.
2. Observe differences in rate of response, confidence, and accuracy.
3. Do not use the alternate language until *after* item 8 is completed, and then only if the first response was very hesitant or was incorrectly given.
4. Have the 6- and 7-year-olds read item A, Part II, in both languages, and record and compare letter responses in *both languages*.

If items 1 though 8 were all answered quickly and correctly, there is no need to restate them in a second language. As indicated, however, if the answers on any of the items were given hesitantly, incorrectly, or not at all, select the appropriate alternate item.

PART II (6-1 to 11 Years)

To prepare for the test, reproduce, cut out, and band together in sets of six the boxed pictures in Appendix I, pages 243-245. Each level or set of cards, I-VI, consists of six cards.

For children of 6-1 to 8 years, start the test with the letter identification task at the beginning of the Part II response sheet, page 61. For children 8 or older begin with the cards.

Ask the student to identify the picture on each card in Spanish or English, whichever comes to mind *first*. Make this request in both English and Spanish at the introduction of the cards, as written on the record sheet, page 61.

NOTE: Typical responses expected may be found on page 62.

Scoring the Test: Guidelines for scoring the test are presented in the following table.

Level	English	Spanish	OPTIMUM	Responses fast and accurate with good pronunciation
Early Childhood			/8	
Letters			/18	
Cards I			/6	
Cards II			/6	
Cards III			/6	
Cards IV			/6	
Cards V			/6	
Cards VI			/6	

At the early childhood level, the highest possible score is 8. The base score is 4. All four questions in Spanish and English earn the optimum 4 points in each language *or* 8 points if totally answered in only one language.

All of the letters read correctly in Spanish and English earn the optimum of 18 points. Based on this test, students should be classed as:

- *bilingual* if the quality and rate of responses are equally good in both languages.
- *English* if the rate of response is more rapid, confidently given, and with better pronunciation than in Spanish.
- *Spanish* if the rate of response is more rapid, confidently given, and with better pronunciation than in English.

In all tests, the rate and confidence with which the response is given are important, but in a language dominance test, these two aspects of quality plus pronunciation are almost on a par with accuracy. Because of the importance of quality, judgments in this test cannot be made by numbers alone.

Remediation: No remediation is necessary when the dominant language matches the language(s) of instruction: English with English, Spanish with Spanish, bilingual with bilingual. In those instances where the language of instruction does not match the student's strengths, he or she needs to be tutored in the language of instruction before and during regular classroom work. Curriculum activities in a bilingual educational program continue to be conducted in both languages, and such a program is appropriate only as the school population warrants this emphasis.

A small percentage of students who lack an *aptitude* for languages are confused and penalized by a bilingual program. These students are most often rated as non-fluent in both languages. Such students need to be tutored in the language in which they are MOST likely to function for the rest of their lives. Conferencing with parents is important in determining the dominant language.

> NOTE: Channeling ALL students of Mexican-American or Puerto Rican descent through totally Spanish instruction is no better than channeling such students through totally English instruction or even through totally bilingual instruction. However, offering such students a diversified program is more likely to meet their needs.

Diversity can be offered only IF the training of the faculty permits. Therefore, it seems logical that schools having a high enrollment of Spanish-speaking students should also have a high percentage of bilingual Spanish-English speaking teachers. Provision should be made to:

- tutor students in either language,
- instruct students in either language, and
- instruct bilingual students in BOTH languages

according to the needs of the students. In other words, the faculty's qualifications should be such as to permit flexibility from semester to semester.

Test 10   *LANGUAGE DOMINANCE, English/Spanish*
LaPray/Casares

Name _____ Grade _____   Chronological Age _____
                                                                        yr.   mo.
Date _____ Examiner _____   Score: _____
Observations _____   English __/8__ Spanish __/8__
_____   Dominant Language _____
_____   Bilingual _____
_____   Equal Non-Fluency _____

PART I   *Ages 4 yrs. 6 mo. to 6 yrs.*

ENGLISH SPANISH   Read items 1 though 8 as written. (Do not use the alternate items until items 1 though 8 have been read to the student.*)

1. What is your name? (Accept single-wd. ans.)
   (Alternate/¿Cómo te llamas?)

2. ¿Donde esta tu nariz? (Enséñame donde está tu nariz.)
   (Alternate/ Point to your nose.)

3. Point to your eyes.
   (Alternate/ Enséñame donde están tus ojos.)

4. Enséñame donde están tus orejas.
   (Alternate/ Point to your ears.)

5. ¿Cuántes años tienes?
   (Alternate/ How old are you?)

6. Can you read this?
   (Print child's name --
   (Alternate/¿Puedes leer esto?)

7. Point to your chin.
   (Alternate/ Enséñame donde está tu barba.)

8. ¿Me puedes escribir tu nombre?
   (Alternate/ Can you write your name? —— from memory?)

*Use alternate items only if the response to the orignal item was very hesitant or was incorrect.

Test 10   LANGUAGE DOMINANCE, English/Spanish
LaPray/Casares

Name _____ Grade_____   Chronological Age _____
                                                                yr.   mo.
Date_____ Examiner_____   Score: _____
Observations _____   English_____Spanish_____
_____   Dominant Language _____
_____   Bilingual _____
_____   Equal Non-Fluency _____

PART II   Ages 6 yrs. 1 mo. to 11 yrs.

A. Letter Identification (Ages 6-1 to 8 yrs.)

_____What letters are these? _____Cuales letras non estas?

A	O	C	A	O	C
F	G	I	F	G	I
B	E	U	B	E	U

B. Picture Identification (Ages 6 through 11)

"Please tell what you see in Spanish or English whichever comes to mind first."
"Dime en español o en inglés de lo que piensas cuando ves este retrato."

CARD SETS

I English/Spanish	II English/Spanish	III English/Spanish
1 ____ ____	7 ____ ____	13 ____ ____
2 ____ ____	8 ____ ____	14 ____ ____
3 ____ ____	9 ____ ____	15 ____ ____
4 ____ ____	10 ____ ____	16 ____ ____
5 ____ ____	11 ____ ____	17 ____ ____
6 ____ ____	12 ____ ____	18 ____ ____

IV	V	VI
19 ____ ____	25 ____ ____	31 ____ ____
20 ____ ____	26 ____ ____	32 ____ ____
21 ____ ____	27 ____ ____	33 ____ ____
22 ____ ____	28 ____ ____	34 ____ ____
23 ____ ____	29 ____ ____	35 ____ ____
24 ____ ____	30 ____ ____	36 ____ ____

Typical Responses to Part II

Level I

1. mom ma mama mother lady woman
   mamá mamacita mujer señorita señora

2. house cottage
   casa casita domicilio

3. one number one numeral one
   uno número uno

4. sun sunshine
   el sol brillo del sol

5. tree (or special type as elm)
   arbol

6. papa dad father man
   papá papacito hombre

Level II

7. white
   blanco

8. ball beachball
   pelota bola

9. N
   N

10. black dark
    negro obscuro

11. 4 four
    cuatro 4

12. pencil marker
    lápiz

Level III

13. 5
    cinco

14. apple
    manzana

15. banana
    plátano

16. L
    L

17. six
    seis

18. spoon teaspoon tablespoon
    cuchara

Level IV

19. M
    M

20. seven
    siete

21. milk
    leche

22 glass
    vaso

23. hand
    mano

24. ten
    diez

Level V

25. hat
    sombrero

26. eleven
    once

27. car auto automobile V/W
    auto carro automóvil

28. cup
    copa taza

29. bookS
    libroS

30. treeS
    árboleS

Level VI

31. twenty
    veinte

32. sailboat boat
    barco de vela

33. umbrella
    paraguas sombrilla

34. thirty
    treinta

35 glasses
    lentes antejos

36. one hundred   a hundred
    cien ciento

Section III Summary

Section III presents five assessment tools, one for monitoring reversals, one for diagnosing reading readiness, two for screening intellectual capacity, and one for screening children of unknown language dominance.

Establishing directionality in letters for beginning readers is essential. Letters often reversed vertically are *p d, M W, n* and *u*. Letters often reversed horizontally are *a b d, q p g, s* and *z*.

In order to prevent students from confusing the following letters, it is advisable to overlearn one before introducing the other. For instance, overlearn *b* before learning *d*, *M* before *W*, and *n* before *u*. However, no matter how many safeguards are built into instruction, it is NOT unusual for some reversals to surface in the primary grades. Reversals that persist through grade 3 are of concern. By this time, with effective instruction, even stubborn directionality problems should be corrected. Test 6, Reversal Letters and Words, is one way of assessing the extent of the reversal problem.

Test 7, Personalized Reading Readiness, assesses readiness in the areas of matching letters, words, and sentences. The only word the child is expected to recognize is his/her own name.

Tests 8 and 9, Non-Verbal Intelligence and Body/Receptive Vocabulary, are two measures of intelligence. In the non-verbal test the student's attention to details of the face and head is scored. In the Body/Receptive Vocabulary the student first listens to the name of the body part and then points to it.

Test 10, Language Dominance English/Spanish, is to be used only when the student's dominant language is undetermined.

References

Crews, Donald. *We Read: A to Z.* New York: Harper & Row, 1967.

Durkin, Dolores. *Teaching Young Children to Read.* Boston: Allyn & Bacon, 1972.

Geisel, Theodore. *Dr. Suess's ABC.* New York: Random House, 1963.

Harris, Dale B. *Children's Drawings as Measures of Intellectual Maturity.* New York: Harcourt Brace Jovanovich, 1963.

Harrison-Stroud. *Reading Readiness Profiles.* Boston: Houghton Mifflin.

Jordan, Brian T. Jordan Left-Right Reversal Test. Rafael, Ca.: Academic Therapy Publications, rev. ed. 1974.

LaPray, Margaret, and Ramon Ross. *A B C and Me.* Chicago: Rand McNally, 1978.

Meeker, Mary. *Structure of the Intellect: Its Interpretation and Uses.* Columbus, Ohio: Merrill, 1969.

Olguin, Leonard. *Shuck Loves Chirley.* San Marino, Ca.: Golden West Publishing House, 1968.

Rey, Hans A. *Curious George Learns the Alphabet.* Boston: Houghton Mifflin, 1963.

Travers, Pamela L. *Mary Poppins From A to Z.* New York: Harcourt Brace Jovanovich, 1962.

Wildsmith, Brian. *A B C.* New York: Franklin Watts, Inc., 1963.

pet /cat

feline
domesticated
animal

ME   *SECTION IV*

measuring letter and word skills

(Contains Tests 11 through 18)

Reading definitions, insofar as they are complete, include comprehension. Consensus, then, leads to the need for developing comprehension through attention to the *unit-bearing* load.

At this point there is disagreement. Goodman and some other linguists insist that it is the *sentence* rather than the *word* that is the unit-bearing load. "No," say the semanticists, "it is the *word* that is the unit-bearing load. It is the *word* through mapping and boundaries that represents acts, objects, and feelings."

Take the word *run*, for example, It has dozens of definitions. Mapped into these general areas of meanings, the branches look something like this:

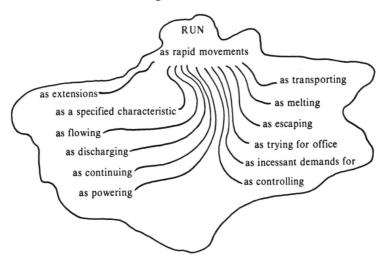

Despite the diverse meanings assigned to *run*, there are limitations or boundaries presently set on this word. Placing the word in a sentence certainly helps us to select a meaning from the boundaries already set. But no matter how we try, by using a neologism, or by whatever ploy, we cannot immediately stretch the word completely outside of present-day usage. Words have grammatical flexibility and limitations as well as meanings that are determined by present-day usage. For example, we cannot use *run* in the following sentences and have the word make sense:

> *Run* John is handsome.
> *Run* are eatable.

Consequently, we can say in agreement with the semanticists that meanings of words can be mapped and that words do have commonly accepted boundaries. We need to assess a student's knowledge of words and word boundaries and we can begin by testing the extent of sight words.

One of the quickest and most productive assessments available to teachers is a graded word list. With a few minutes' time, the graded word list helps the teacher gather the following information:

(on achievement)	1. reading grade level	(independent
(on confidence)	2. speed of recognition	instructional
	3. volume in pronunciation	frustration
(on phonics)	4. strengths in word recognition (initial, medial, final)	
(on sight words)	5. words known	
	6. words not known	

Were teachers limited to the use of ONLY two tests in the area of reading, one should be a graded word list, and the other an oral paragraph test preferably including the same words as on the graded word list. The San Diego Quick Assessment is such a test. Furthermore, by alternating Forms I and II of the San Diego Quick Assessment, the student's progress can be recorded using Form I at the beginning and end of the year, and Form II during the mid-year.

Because of the importance of assessing sight words, the two forms of the San Diego Quick Assessment are placed first in this section. However, all of the tests found in the section are designed to assess decoding or word comprehension. The following Test Guide (Table V) serves as a quick reference to all of the tests in the section.

Table V
Test Guide 11-18

	Test	Title	Ages	Minutes	Appropriate for
D E C O D I N G	11-12	San Diego Quick Assessment Forms I and II	5-16	3	screening for reader level at kindergarten through grade 11
	13	Applied Phonics	6-10	15	students with a meager sight vocabulary and poor word attack skills
	14	Structural Analysis	6-12	15	students with meager vocabularies
C O M P R E H E N S I O N	15	Word Opposites	5-16	5	students with poor comprehension of antonyms
	16	Typical Uses or Locations	6	10	students with poor comprehension and limited vocabularies
	17	Word Relationships	7-14	5	students who score low in comprehension
	18	Word Sets	6-14	10	students who are careless and who tend to miscall words

Throughout these tests no attempt is made to isolate sounds or to test through *nonsense* syllables. For predicting future performance, it seems most logical to test within the same context in which the student is expected to perform daily.

All of the tests in this section are MAINLY aimed at word pronunciation and comprehension. In a few instances, sentences are included to check on the student's ability to apply what he knows. This test of application is an expedient measure and the sentences themselves are only of secondary importance.

Tests 11 and 12   SAN DIEGO QUICK ASSESSMENT (SDQA)

Forms I and II

Description: Beginning with the three readiness levels of recognizing letters as similar, saying letter names, and matching sounds to letters, this test proceeds to recognition of words. Words for the test were selected from the Thorndike-Century Dictionary and from three basic reader series published by Ginn, Rand McNally, and Scott Foresman, respectively. They were tried out in classrooms in San Diego County and adjusted for level of difficulty.

Appropriate for: students at the end of summer vacation, or for new students entering the classroom without recent or detailed records.

Ages: 5-16, or older students with learning disabilities.

Testing Time: 2 minutes.

Directions for Use:
   Preparation: For this test you will need copies of 32 boxed cards, 16 for Form I (Appendix II, pages 246-250) and 16 for Form II (Appendix III, pages 251-255). You can simply cut out the cards on the boxed lines or reproduce them from the pages of the *File*. Sequence the cards in this order: I RR^1, I RR^2, I RR^3, I-1 — I-13; II RR^1, II RR^2, II RR^3, II-1 — II-13. Then place the cards for each form in a separate photographic album so they can be easily flipped over as completed.

   You will also need copies of the SDQA record sheets for the form to be used. Form I sheets are found on pages 71 and 72, and Form II sheets on pages 73 and 74.

Administration: Administer each form of the SDQA individually, as follows:

   1. Start at one grade level below the one in which the child is presently enrolled, and adjust the difficulty up or down according to the student's responses.
   2. Place one card at a time in front of the student.
   3. Direct the child as follows, and place a checkmark (✓) at the appropriate entry on the record sheet for each two-second hesitation:

   RR^1: "Which letters are alike?"
   RR^2: "Name these letters."
   RR^3: "Circle the letter you think this word begins with."
   I-13: ● "Read as many of the words on this list as you can."
   　　● "Try to sound out words that are new to you."
   　　● "Don't be afraid to tell me ANY part of a word that you recognize."
   　　● "Each list gets harder. You won't be able to recognize all of the words, but
   　　　do the best you can."

Scoring the Test:

Simplified Scoring: Simplified scoring of the SDQA includes two measures:

1. Substitutions are written in and analyzed as to the position of errors: initial, medial, or final.
2. Two errors on one list establishes the student's instructional level.

Detailed Scoring: For more detailed scoring:

1. Raw score is computed by allowing 10 points for every list correctly read and 10 points for every list below this level:

For example:

Student A who is in third grade begins by reading ALL of the second-grade list correctly. He therefore is given 10 points for the second-grade list and 60 points for the lists preceding:

$$
\begin{array}{rcl}
RR^1 & - & 10 \\
RR^2 & - & 10 \\
RR^3 & - & 10 \\
1—Pre\ Pr & - & 10 \\
2—Primer & - & 10 \\
3—First & - & \underline{10} \\
& & 60 + 10 = 70
\end{array}
$$

Student A passed 8 words on the third-grade list. He then missed the first 2 words on the fourth-grade list. He said the third word correctly, but missed the fourth word. At this point testing may be terminated. Scoring is as follows:

$$
\begin{array}{l}
70 \text{ for previous lists} \\
8 \text{ for third grade} \\
\underline{1 \text{ for the fourth-grade list}} \\
79 \text{ Raw Score}
\end{array}
$$

	Raw score	Independent reader level	Instructional reader level	Frustration reader level
Pretest	79	2.0	3.0	4.0
Posttest	86	2.0	3.0	5.0

On the retest given two months later this child still tested 3.0 for the instructional level, but the raw score is 86 or *7 words more* and the frustration level is raised to grade 5.0. In addition, the substitutions were closer to the correct word on the posttest, for example: in the first test *served* for *several* and in the retest *severed* for *several.* In the first instance a one-syllable word was substituted for a three-syllable word in the test, while in the posttest the first two sounds of the word are correct.

2. Two errors on one list establishes the student's instructional level.
3. One error on a list or no errors on the list preceding the instructional list is considered the independent level.

4. To be sure the misses were not happenstance, it is wise to give the student the next list above the instructional level. If on the list the first three words are missed, there is no need for further testing. If, on the other hand, the next list is ALL correct and only two words on the list above the perfect one are missed, consider the instructional level as the FIRST list on which the child missed two. This is a conservative decision and is more likely to result in successes than choosing the higher of the two lists for instructional purposes.
5. Frustration level is any list with 3 or more errors.

Remediation: The type of errors noted in the word substitutions dictates the remediation to be used. For example, students who consistently miss words by starting the word incorrectly:

> toad for road
> give for live
> digger for bigger
> right for night

need exercises stressing initial consonants. This is equally true of medial and final errors.

Remediation should ALWAYS involve the largest unit possible. For example, the child who substitutes *think* for *thank* could be taught the medial vowel sound of $\breve{a}$ in place of $\breve{i}$, but it is a more economical unit to teach the *ank* as it rhymes in *bank, tank, crank,* etc. In the English language, short vowels never appear isolated.

Test 11 SAN DIEGO QUICK ASSESSMENT FORM I

Name _____ Grade _____

Date of Test _____ Examiner _____

Observations: _____

_____

Chronological Age _____

yr.   mo.

SDQA Grade Level _____

Raw Score _____

RR¹			RR²		RR³	
B	B		B		D B A	(bird)
A	C		A		A E K	(apron)
M	M		M		L F M	(mom)
C	C		C		B C G	(car)
S	Q		S		O S P	(sad)
J	J		J		A B J	(jeep)
T	T		T		D G T	(tag)
H	H		H		A H B	(house)
D	L		D		D I M	(door)
W	M		W		W G J	(wig)

1   PP

see _____

play _____

me _____

at _____

run _____

go _____

and _____

look _____

can _____

here _____

2   Primer

you _____

come _____

not _____

with _____

jump _____

help _____

is _____

work _____

are _____

this _____

3

road _____

live _____

thank _____

when _____

bigger _____

how _____

always _____

night _____

spring _____

today _____

4

our _____

please _____

myself _____

town _____

early _____

send _____

wide _____

believe _____

quietly _____

carefully _____

5

city _____

middle _____

moment _____

frightened _____

exclaimed _____

several _____

lonely _____

drew _____

since _____

straight _____

6

decided _____

served _____

amazed _____

silent _____

wrecked _____

improve _____

certainly _____

entered _____

realized _____

interrupted _____

Test 11   SDQA I (cont.)

7

scanty _____
business _____
develop _____
considered _____
discussed _____
behaved _____
splendid _____
acquainted _____
escape _____
grim _____

8

bridge _____
commercial _____
abolish _____
trucker _____
apparatus _____
elementary _____
comment _____
necessity _____
gallery _____
relativity _____

9

amber _____
dominion _____
sundry _____
capillary _____
impetuous _____
blight _____
wrest _____
enumerate _____
daunted _____
condescend _____

10

capacious _____
limitations _____
pretext _____
intrigue _____
delusions _____
immaculate _____
ascent _____
acrid _____
binoculars _____
embankment _____

11

conscientious _____
isolation _____
molecule _____
ritual _____
momentous _____
vulnerable _____
kinship _____
conservatism _____
jaunty _____
inventive _____

12

zany _____
jerkin _____
nausea _____
gratuitous _____
linear _____
inept _____
legality _____
aspen _____
amnesty _____
barometer _____

13

galore _____
rotunda _____
capitalism _____
prevaricate _____
risible _____

exonerate _____
superannuate _____
luxuriate _____
piebald _____
crunch _____

Test 12   SAN DIEGO QUICK ASSESSMENT   FORM II

Name _____ Grade _____   Chronological Age _____

Date of Test _____ Examiner _____   yr.   mo.

Observations: _____   SDQA Grade Level _____

_____   Raw Score _____

_____

RR¹	H	L	RR²	D	RR³	A	L	D	(dandy)
	A	A		K		K	L	M	(kite)
	N	M		N		W	N	G	(needle)
	D	D		B		B	D	M	(battle)
	S	L		J		C	L	J	(jam)
	W	M		L		F	L	N	(lamp)
	F	F		W		A	W	E	(window)
	D	B		Y		H	O	Y	(yard)
	K	K		A		A	H	B	(ape)
	Y	Y		F		F	E	Q	(farm)

1   PP

red _____

jump _____

be _____

it _____

ran _____

come _____

to _____

I _____

ride _____

book _____

2   Primer

he _____

wants _____

no _____

the _____

find _____

home _____

will _____

too _____

was _____

them _____

3

load _____

give _____

banks _____

ten _____

from _____

now _____

almost _____

winter _____

Monday _____

white _____

4

your _____

track _____

herself _____

dance _____

ear _____

back _____

dark _____

received _____

quite _____

bravely _____

5

cent _____

riddles _____

movement _____

light _____

reclaim _____

grade _____

alone _____

few _____

already _____

eight _____

6

reside _____

curves _____

famous _____

violent _____

wrong _____

important _____

surely _____

centered _____

returned _____

science _____

Test 12   SDQA II (cont.)

7

shape _____

blaze _____

defeated _____

consider _____

distress _____

bicycle _____

splendor _____

acquired _____

escort _____

interplay _____

8

breach _____

financial _____

polished _____

lucky _____

crimes _____

opposite _____

lament _____

security _____

notable _____

ignorance _____

9

torment _____

provision _____

dainty _____

stationary _____

frontier _____

flight _____

wrist _____

ambitious _____

marsh _____

descend _____

10

alfalfa _____

savor _____

biscuits _____

contrary _____

deign _____

firmament _____

gymnasium _____

insanity _____

flaunted _____

protoplasm _____

11

concentrate _____

immunity _____

secondary _____

crevice _____

cascade _____

spur _____

reverberate _____

solitary _____

lulled _____

fanatical _____

12

trance _____

enterprise _____

querulous _____

interval _____

technique _____

vegetarian _____

replenishing _____

obscurely _____

compulsion _____

verbatim _____

13

recumbent _____

ominously _____

diminishing _____

soliloquy _____

incandescence _____

meditations _____

deprecating _____

provender _____

terrapins _____

terminate _____

Test 13   APPLIED PHONICS

Description: This test includes a sampling of consonants, phonograms, single syllables, syllable codes, and blanks to be filled in by the student. Specifically, the sampling includes:

- Initial consonants p, t, g, r, m / s, f, b, c, h
- Consonant clusters pl, wh, gr, pr, sm / cr, th, gl, ch, tr
- Phonograms an, en, in, od, ug / ane, ete, ide, oke, uge
- Short and long vowels in phonograms
- One- and two-syllable words
- Endings /n/ /k/ /l/ /ө/ /č
- Sentences — decoding in content
- Sounds of c and g
- Syllabication codes

Appropriate for: students who are considered non-fluent readers, who score considerably below their grade level on the San Diego Quick Assessment.

Ages: 6-10, or older students with a reading disability.

Testing Time: 15 minutes.

Directions for Use:

Administer the test individually, as follows:

1. Give the student a copy of the "Student's Form" for the test, on pages 78 and 79, to complete as you read the directions from the "Examiner Record Form," page 77.
2. Mark the student's responses on the examiner's form.
3. Give help as needed in pronouncing the phonograms in isolation. However, be sure to record that assistance was given.
4. For economy of time *do not* continue testing if the student misses all or even MOST of the initial consonants. Since testing is mainly for assessing needs, these have already been targeted. To subject the student to total failure is unnecessary.

Scoring the Test: Answers are on the examiner's form. The highest possible total raw score is 86. However, this test's greatest help is in pinpointing the student's strengths and needs. Those areas needing reteaching can be assessed by glancing over the test to see in which category the errors fall.

Remediation: Since English words are read from *left* to *right,* the initial sounds are always the first needed to figure out words. Therefore, if the student misses items 2, 5, 8, 11, and 14, testing should be discontinued and these initial consonants should be taught.

For students who miss items 3, 6, 9, 12, and 15, one plan is to start by teaching words like *pl*ant, *wh*ack, *g*rant, *pr*actice and *sm*ack.

For students who miss items 21, 24, 27, 30, and 33, try teaching sat, pat, rat, cat, hat.

For children who miss 22, 25, 28, 31, and 34, crab, that, glad, chap, trap.

If errors are made mainly in filling in the blanks, activities similar to those missed should be selected from phonics workbooks or should be made up by the teacher.

Students who miss the syllabication codes should be given sufficient practice to learn those codes, selecting one of Kottmeyer's appropriate-level spelling books and/or showing a Kottmeyer filmstrip. (See "References" at the end of this section.)

Test 13. *APPLIED PHONICS — Examiner Record Form (Answer Sheet)*

Name _____ Grade _____   Chronological Age _____
                                                                    yr.   mo.
Date of Test _____ Examiner _____   + strengths — needs help
Observations: _____   consonants _____ c
_____   phonograms _____ 9
_____   fill in _____ syllables _____

Draw a line *under* the correct grapheme and *through* the incorrect one.

A B̸   (A is correct; B̸ is incorrect.)

I. Read items 1 through 15. Try them all; guess if you need to.

Phonograms	1 an	4 en	7 in	10 od	13 ug
Consonants	2 p	5 t	8 g	11 r	14 m
C. Clusters	3 pl	6 wh	9 gr	12 pr	15 sm

Fill in the blanks with a word from 1 through 15 that makes sense.

16 plan   18 when
17 grin   19 mug

II. Try items 20 through 24.

Phonograms	20 ane	23 ete	26 ide	29 oke	32 uge
	21 s	24 P	27 r	30 c	33 h
	22 cr	25 th	28 gl	31 ch	34 tr

Fill in the blanks with a word from 20 through 34 that makes sense.

35 These   37 crane
36 true   38 ride

III. Try items 39 through 58.

Phonograms	39 ank	43 ink	47 unk	51 at	55 ack
	40 b	44 l	48 d	52 h	56 b
	41 th	45 br	49 shr	53 fl	57 sh
	42 blanket	46 drinking	50 sunken	54 platter	58 cracker

Fill in the blanks with a word from 39 through 58 that makes sense.

59 platter   61 Drinking   63 sunken
60 blanket   62 cracker

IV Try 64 through 68.

Endings   64 cone /n/   65 desk /k/   66 bell /l/   67 tenth /θ/   68 church /č/

V Try these syllables and words 69 through 80.

Sounds of c and g
(single syllables)

69 cir	73 geo	77 circus	80 gym
70 car̈	74 gio	78 cattle	
71 cer	75 gag	79 garage	
72 cur	76 got		

VI Syllabication Codes. Mark the division and write the code beside the word as in examples.

Examples			
city _____ v/cv	81 dentist _____ vc/cv	84 body _____ v/cv	
handle _____ /c le	82 unit _____ v/cv	85 able _____ /c le	
basket _____ vc/cv	83 jolly _____ vc/cv	86 cotton _____ vc/cv	

Test 13   APPLIED PHONICS — *Student's Form*

I. "Read the following aloud."

1. an	4. en	7. in	10. od	13. ug
2. pan	5. ten	8. gin	11. rod	14. mug
3. plan	6. when	9. grin	12. prod	15. smug

"Fill in the blanks with the words or combination from above."

16. This pl _____ is a good one.

17. Gr _____ if you like this joke.

18. Wh _____ you finish eating, we will work.

19. I'll drink from this m_____.

II.

20. ane	23. ete	26. ide	29. oke	32. uge
21. sane	24. Pete	27. ride	30. coke	33. huge
22. crane	25. these	28. glide	31. choke	34. true

35. Th _____ books are new.

36. What I told you is tr_____.

37. A cr _____ is a bird with long legs.

38. I will r _____ my bike.

III.

39. ank	43. ink	47. unk	51. at	55. ack
40. bank	44. link	48. dunk	52. hat	56. back
41. thank	45. brink	49. shrunk	53. flat	57. shack
42. blanket	46. drinking	50. sunken	54. platter	58. cracker

59. Put the turkey on this pl _____ .

60. The bl _____ goes on the bed.

61. Dr _____ four glasses of water a day is healthy.

62. Here is a cr _____ to go with the soup.

63. A s _____ ship could have treasures.

Test 13 Student's Form (cont.)

IV. Example: tub/tub/b/
64. cone   65. desk   66. bell   67. tenth   68. church

V.

69. cir   72. cur   75. gag   78. cattle
70. car   73. geo   76. got   79. garage
71. cer   74. gio   77. circus   80. gym

VI.

Examples:	
ci/ty	v/cv
han/dle	/c le
bas/ket	vc/cv

81. dentist _____   84. body _____
82. unit _____   85. able _____
83. jolly _____   86. cotton _____

Test 14 STRUCTURAL ANALYSIS

Description: This test includes: compound words
endings: s, ed, ing, er, est, ful, fully, less, lessness
prefixes: in, sub, trans
root words: aqua, graph, ology, cycle
words in context

Appropriate for: students who tend to miscall words and word endings.

Ages: 6-12.

Testing Time: 15 minutes.

Directions for Use:
Test 13 should precede this test. In fact, if the student does poorly on the Applied Phonics Test, do not administer this test until he or she learns the basic decoding skills.
Administer the SA individually, giving the student a copy of the test form on pages 82 and 83.

Scoring the Test: Answers for parts II, III, V, VI, and VII of the test are provided in the key below. The total possible score is 74. However, more important than the raw score is the pattern of strengths and weaknesses that emerges.

Remediation: Select a structural analysis work book from Barnell and Loft or another commercial source. Use worksheets such as those found in *Structural Analysis Activity Sheets,* a collection of duplicating masters for grades 2-6 published by The Center for Applied Research in Education. Or design your own activities similar to the ones in which the student experiences difficulty.

Answer Key

II.
1. planting	4. camped	7. stripes
2. plants	5. camping	8. striped
3. planted	6. camp	9. stripes

10. plotted	13. rules, ruled
11. plot	14. ruled
12. plots	15. ruling

III. 16. good
      17. better
      18. best

V.   39. transport
      40. infield
      41. subtract
      42. subway
      43. transcribe, inscribe, subscribe
      44. invent
      45. transact, inact
      46. inlet, sublet
      47. inside, subside

VI.   48. nervous
      49. government
      50. reference
      51. ridiculous
      52. excitement
      53. zealous
      54. famous
      55. argument

VII. 56. water
      57. something written
      58. circle, wheel
      59. blue-green
      60. a board towed behind a boat for a rider
      61. a glass tank container
      62. a picture
      63. a record player
      64. written, drawn
      65. two-wheeled vehicle
      66. a storm
      67. a three-wheeled vehicle
      68. study of plants and animals
      69. study of mind and behavior
      70. study of animals and animal life

VIII. 71. Aquamarine
      72. photograph
      73. bicycle
      74. Zoology

Test 14   STRUCTURAL ANALYSIS

Name _____ Grade _____   Chronological Age _____

	yr.	mo.
compounds	_____ context	____
endings	_____ TOTAL	__/74
prefixes		
root words		

Date of Test _____ Examiner _____
Observation: _____
_____
_____

I. Pronounce these compound words.
   1. doghouse   3. goldfish   5. backpacking
   2. trademark   4. junkyard   6. raincoat

II. Fill in the blanks with the word in the box using the correct endings of s, ed, and ing.

| plant |
1. I will be _____ flowers tonight.
2. How many _____ do we have?
3. I _____ one rose yesterday.

| camp |
4. Have you ever _____ before?
5. I have gone _____ since I was young.
6. I own four _____ stools.

| stripes |
7. His shirt has _____ .
8. Her dress is _____ .
9. The wallpaper has _____ on the border.

| plot |
10. He _____ to run away on Friday.
11. A story has a _____ .
12. Books have _____ to make them interesting.

| rule |
13. The Queen _____ her country.
14. The King _____ before he died.
15. The _____ class is becoming less popular.

III. Fill in the correct words. *good   best   better*
   16. The youngest in the family is a _____ player.
   17. The second son is _____ than the youngest.
   18. The third son is the _____ player in the whole family.

Test 14 (cont.)

IV. Read the following words:

19 care	24 thought
20 careful	25 thoughtful
21 carefully	26 thoughtfully
22 careless	27 thoughtless
23 carelessness	28 thoughtlessness

29 grace	34 taste
30 graceful	35 tasteful
31 gracefully	36 tastefully
32 listless	37 tasteless
33 listlessness	38 tastelessness

V. Make another word by adding a prefix: _in, sub, trans_

Examples: <u>in</u> to   39 _____ port   42 _____ way   45 _____ act
           <u>sub</u> marine   40 _____ field   43 _____ scribe 46 _____ let
           <u>trans</u> late   41 _____ tract   44 _____ vent   47 _____ side

VI. Make another word by adding a suffix: ment, ous, ence.

Example:

apart<u>ment</u>

48 nerv _____	52 excite _____
48 govern _____	53 zeal _____
50 refer _____	54 fam _____
51 ridicul _____	55 argu _____

VII. Give the meaning of the following root-words or words:

56 aqua _____
57 graph _____
58 cycle _____

59 aquamarine	62 photograph	65 bicycle	68 biology
60 aquaplane	63 phonograph	66 cyclone	69 psychology
61 aquarium	64 graphic	67 tricycle	70 zoology

VIII. Fill in the blank spaces with the words from VII.

71. _____ is my favorite color.
72. I developed a _____ that I took with my own camera.
73. When I was two I had a tricycle but now I ride a _____ .
74. _____ is a study of animals and animal life.

Test 15   GRADED WORD OPPOSITES

Description: In this test of word opposites the stimulus word is always given orally by the examiner. The student then selects a word from the multiple choice given that he considers opposite in meaning. The test consists of 8 words at each grade level beginning with primer and extending through grade eleven. (See pages 86-90.)

Appropriate for: students of at least primer level reading ability through eleventh grade. It is particularly useful for students with average or better intelligence but below average in comprehension of orally or silently read materials.

Ages: 5-16, or older students with reading disabilities.

Testing Time: 5 minutes.

Directions for Use:

Administer the test individually, or in small groups.

1. Give the student a copy of the test, pages 86-90, and ask him to read aloud (or underline, if used with a group) the word opposite in meaning to the word read to him.
2. Be sure to establish that the child knows the *meaning* of the word opposite.
3. Start at one grade level below the student's present grade and adjust the difficulty up or down.

Oral directions are as follows:

- "Read (or mark) the word opposite in meaning to the word I tell you."
- "In working through the example you will note that the answer is to be found in one of a multiple choice."
- "Each word list gets harder, but do the best you can."

Scoring the Test: An answer key for this test is provided below. In scoring the test:

1. Raw score is the total correctly identified plus 8 points for each list below any list TOTALLY correct.
2. Two errors on any one list establishes the grade level for understanding word opposites. This is considered the instructional level.

Remediation: In those instances in which the student gives the correct answer but marks the wrong word, the problem is one of learning to identify words and has nothing to do with understanding word opposites. For example, the examiner says *little* and the child says *big,* but marks *boy.*

In clear-cut cases where the student does not know most of the opposites, exercises can be devised or found to teach these concepts:

- Is it a big ball? No, it is a little ball.
- Is it a big hamburger? No, it is a little hamburger.
- Is she rich? No, she is poor.
- Is an elephant tiny? No, an elephant is large.
- Are frogs pretty? No, frogs are ugly.
- Are worms pretty? No, worms are ugly.

Grade Level	Answer Key
Pr.	likes, sit, up, big, in, went, happy, cannot
1	boys, fast, woman, drop, his, day, found, good
2	first, right, light, quiet, open, front, round, hello
3	afraid, gentle, hard, silly, awake, west, less, stood
4	bold, least, mine, able, true, smoothly, forget, king
5	fake, entrance, inner, strong, soaked, awful, direct, finished
6	beautiful, expensive, frown, dull, difficult, advanced, generous, public
7	cowardly, immature, rested, stiff, graceful, industrious, oral, untidy
8	strengthen, uncle, criticize, illegal, failure, ascend, intellectual, original
9	rejected, tense, boastful, automatic, brunette, poverty, disperse, extravagant
10	murky, insecure, raze, obese, exterior, turbulent, maternal, vulgar
11	nonflammable, pliable, vacuous, inarticulate, agile, shy, obvious, indulge

Test 15　GRADED WORD OPPOSITES

Name _____ Grade _____　Chronological Age _____

Date of Test _____ Examiner _____　yr.　mo.

Grade Level _____

Observations _____　Raw Score _____

_____　Average _____

_____　Above _____ Below _____

EXAMPLE: Examiner says: *walk.*　　　Student silently marks or responds aloud:

(Help the student, but ONLY if necessary.)　　boy　run　see

HATES	likes	jump	look
STAND	see	was	sit
DOWN	you	at	up
LITTLE	boy	big	bad
OUT	in	its	is
CAME	was	went	were
SAD	happy	house	have
CAN	no	car	cannot

GIRLS	bump	boys	baby
SLOW	fast	seesaw	hop
MAN	pole	window	woman
LIFT	drop	step	bear
HERS	foot	his	rain
NIGHT	day	dark	down
LOST	button	found	please
BAD	candy	and	good

LAST	fist	fast	first
LEFT	red	right	round
DARK	light	low	leave
NOISY	quiet	stand	silly
CLOSE	oven	over	open
BACK	from	front	free
SQUARE	rosy	round	read
GOODBYE	hello	help	hold

FEARLESS	after	over	afraid
ROUGH	gone	grow	gentle
SOFT	had	head	hard
SERIOUS	squeal	silly	jeep
ASLEEP	awake	away	always
EAST	with	west	word
MORE	less	lead	load
SAT	said	stood	was

SHY	bold	bad	burn
MOST	level	least	ledge
YOURS	maybe	me	mine
UNABLE	art	able	after
FALSE	trial	throb	true
ROUGHLY	smoothly	stride	slope
REMEMBER	fierce	ferry	forget
QUEEN	king	kept	kite

Test 15   (cont.)

REAL	flat	fake	tough
EXIT	scout	ancient	entrance
OUTER	inner	flow	ramps
WEAK	folks	model	strong
DRIED	soaked	scoop	hedge
WONDERFUL	details	awful	awkward
INDIRECT	firm	queer	direct
INCOMPLETE	fine	finished	firm

UGLY	nice	beautiful	mean
CHEAP	expand	expert	expensive
SMILE	frown	from	freed
BRIGHT	dump	dull	shine
EASY	difficult	needed	swift
PRIMARY	vantage	goal	advanced
STINGY	giant	generous	loose
PRIVATE	public	puncture	please

HEROIC	cowardly	catch	weary
MATURE	immature	model	mauve
WEARY	crowds	crash	rested
FLEXIBLE	styled	stiff	certain
CLUMSY	brief	scar	graceful
LAZY	include	industrious	indolent
WRITTEN	oral	graphic	sonic
NEAT	unfair	untidy	unsure

WEAKEN	close	clarify	strengthen
AUNT	uncle	cousin	relative
PRAISE	admire	criticize	choose
LEGAL	illegal	illspent	illusion
SUCCESS	failure	foil	furnish
DESCEND	derive	ascend	slanted
STUPID	wistful	intellectual	dull
COPY	original	origin	orange

ACCEPTED	rejected	refer	wrapped
RELAXED	joined	tense	fencing
MODEST	boastful	burnt	banter
MANUAL	autograph	automatic	automobile
BLOND	brunette	fair	fortune
WEALTH	rich	poverty	powerful
UNIFY	disperse	divert	divulge
MISERLY	extravagant	extra	stingy

CLEAR	morose	murky	mafia
CONFIDENT	scurvy	secure	insecure
BUILD	raze	razor	route
THIN	obdurate	obese	opal
INTERIOR	exterior	extreme	extol
CALM	turbine	turbulent	trudging
PATERNAL	prefer	morose	maternal
REFINED	vulture	valve	vulgar

Test 15   *(cont.)*

INFLAMMABLE	nonflammable	burnable	safety
OBSTINATE	placate	pliable	play
FULL	vacuous	replete	glutted
FLUENT	inarticulate	articulate	arty
CLUMSY	agate	agent	agile
INTREPID	bold	shy	brave
OBSCURE	obvious	obdurate	obnoxious
ABSTAIN	inhale	injure	indulge

Test 16   TYPICAL USES OR LOCATIONS

Description: This is a test of nouns in typical or broad uses. In some instances, the location or place where the nouns are most often seen is called for. The items are written as multiple choices. (See pages 93-98.)

Appropriate for: students who did poorly on Test 15 and who have low comprehension scores.

Ages: 6 through 16, or older students who have poor comprehension scores.

Testing Time: 10 minutes.

Directions for Use:

1. Provide the student with a copy of the test (pages 93-98) and work through the example first.
2. Start the student at one grade level below his actual grade placement except for second-grade students who will have to begin at second grade.
3. Have students who miss no more than one item out of 8, progress to the next higher level.
4. Test students who miss 2 or more items on the next easier level to establish a basal level.

Scoring the Test: Answers to Test 16 are found on page 92. Directions for scoring are as follows:
1. Designate the level at which 2 out of 8 are missed as the student's instructional level.
2. Keep a record of the total raw score.
3. If possible, establish a *base* level with NO errors. Students are given FULL credit for all items below their base level.

For example:

Student A in the tenth grade started the test at the ninth-grade level and made NO errors.

Base Level 9th grade   8 items

Give credit for ALL the preceding grades, or 8 × 7 = 56.

$$\begin{array}{r} 8 \\ \underline{56} \\ 64 \end{array}$$

At the tenth grade A missed two: +6
At the eleventh grade A missed two also: +6.

$$\begin{array}{r} 64 \\ \underline{+12} \\ 76 \end{array}$$

Instructional level 10th grade

Remediation: Assuming that Student A in the preceding example has average intelligence, scores on this test are as expected. However, had A missed 2 out of 8 on the ninth-grade list, the instructional level of grade 9 would be one grade level below A's expected reading level.

Extended testing may be used, particularly when a student performs below an expected level on this test.

Answer Key

2.

to eat
to play with
as a pet
in a zoo
catch mice
for water
in fairy tales
in school

3.

to drink
to cut
to eat with
to brighten
to see out
after day
to cook on
to play with

4.

to read
to cover
to cool a drink
in a zoo
to warm us
in the country
to drive on
to disturb us

5.

to inform us
as transportation
for education
to fire
for swift travel
for fastening
in the tropics
for packaging

6.

place to catch fish
to test new designs
to explore space
in Indian tribes
for metals
for reading
for transportation
for decorations

7.

haunt houses
transport goods
span valleys
for beauty
in all words
in most words
for rock concerts
for shooting baskets

8.

to pierce a hole
to whip up things
to cover a floor
to entertain
as a string instrument
in hospitals
in transportation
in our solar system

9.

to prevent erosion
inexpensive transportation
designs structures
to entertain
to play in bands
to study the stars
to study plants and animals
within our solar system

10.

draws building plans
chips wood or stone
in chords
in string quartets
studies animals
at mental health clinics
found underwater
to color hair red

11.

found hibernating in winter
to eat
observes and plots stars
to smooth rough wood
found on valentines
in an orchestra
found in college
studies the nervous system

Test 16   TYPICAL USES OR LOCATIONS

Name _____ Grade _____   Chronological Age_____
                                                        yr.   mo.
Date of Test_____ Examiner _____   Total Correct _____
Observations: _____   Present Grade Level _____
_____   TU/L Reader Level _____

Select a typical or broad use for the word given or a typical location. Often there will be more than one correct answer, but you must pick what you consider to be the BEST answer.

Example: "Select the BEST answer."

        homes –––to swim in _____
                to live in_____
                to dress in_____

(Yes, homes are used to dress in, but the BEST answer — the broadest and most typical use of homes — is *to live in.*)

LEVEL 2

food–––to play_____   cats–––catch balls_____
        to drink_____   catch mice_____
        to eat_____   catch colds_____

toys––––to ride in_____   pail––––for water_____
        to play with_____   for eating_____
        to read from_____   for bricks_____

canary–––as a climber_____ giant––––in books_____
          as a pet_____   in fairy tales_____
          as a swimmer_____   in stories_____

lion––––in a bowl_____   students--in school_____
        in a zoo_____   in swimming_____
        in a fire_____   in a kitchen_____

Test 16 *(cont.)*

LEVEL 3

milk - - - to drink_____   window - - to see trees_____
        to eat_____   to see out_____
        to play _____   to play with_____

knife - - -to saw with_____   night - - - -high noon_____
        to cut with_____   before noon_____
        to pound with_____   after day_____

spoon - - to drink with_____   stove - - - to heat_____
        to play with_____   to refrigerate_____
        to eat with_____   to cook on_____

color - - - to brighten_____   marbles - -to play with _____
        to roughen_____   to dribble_____
        to toughen _____   to quiet_____

LEVEL 4

book - - -to copy_____   sun - - - -to wake us_____
        to read_____   to warm us _____
        to memorize_____   to tell time_____

paint - -to float_____   farm - - - in the city_____
        to paper_____   in the country_____
        to cover _____   in dense areas_____

ice - - - -to chip off_____   road - - - to walk on_____
        to swim in_____   to drive on _____
        to cool a drink _____   to camp on_____

giraffe--in a zoo_____   noise- - - -to soothe us_____
        in a show _____   to entertain us _____
        in a circus _____   to disturb us_____

Test 16 (cont.)

LEVEL 5

topic – – – to bore us _____
            to inform us _____
            to warm us _____

car – – – as transparent _____
         as opaque _____
         as transportation _____

school – – for discipline _____
         for education _____
         for adjudication _____

gun – – – to fire _____
         to burn _____
         to dismantle _____

airplane – – for swift travel _____
           for leisure travel _____
           for transportation _____

buttons – – for openness _____
           for dapper looks _____
           for fastening _____

jungle – – – in Antarctica _____
          in the tropics _____
          in Alaska _____

boxes – – – for presents _____
         for tooth picks _____
         for packaging _____

LEVEL 6

lake – – – place to look at _____
        place to catch fish _____
        place to sketch _____

models – – to test new designs _____
         to practice skills _____
         to impress teachers _____

astronaut – to explore atmosphere _____
         to explore oceans _____
         to explore space _____

chiefs – – in Hollywood _____
        in Indian tribes _____
        in Yugoslavia _____

mines – – – for metals _____
        for gold bars _____
        for silver bullion _____

library – – for writing _____
         for reading _____
         for conversing _____

ferry – – – for transportation _____
        for shopping _____
        for cavorting _____

jewelry – – for tranquility _____
         for ballast _____
         for decorations _____

Test 16 (cont.)

LEVEL 7

ghosts____haunt prey_____   vowels ____in some syllables_____
          haunt gems_____   in ALL words_____
          haunt houses_____   in some words_____

truckers___transport milk_____   consonants__in ALL words _____
         transport goods_____   in most words _____
         transport fish_____   in ALL syllables_____

bridges__span valleys_____   guitars____for rock concerts_____
         span oceans_____   for fiddling _____
         span trivia _____   as percussion _____

wigs____for beauty _____   basketball__for hitting homers _____
      for comfort_____   for covering bases _____
      for warmth_____   for shooting baskets_____

LEVEL 8

drill_____to pierce a hole _____   violin ____as percussion _____
      to fasten boards _____   as a string instrument_____
      to smooth boards_____   as a wind instrument _____

beater ___to liquify _____   physician__in hospitals _____
      to whip up things _____   in homes _____
      to smooth boards _____   in schools _____

rug____to dress a wall _____   cyclists____in deliveries _____
     to beautify a room_____   in transportation_____
     to cover a floor _____   in annual races _____

band____to entertain _____   earth ____in our solar system_____
      to play a campus_____   in the cosmos _____
      to gain attention _____   in the Milky Way _____

Test 16   (cont.)

LEVEL 9

plantings _ _to prevent erosion _____
         to prevent washouts _____
         to prevent stagnation _____

motorcycle inexpensive transportation_____
         clean wheels _____
         safe transportation _____

architect_ _designs homes _____
         designs structures _____
         designs shops_____

orchestra_ _to practice _____
         to rehearse _____
         to entertain _____

saxophones_to play in bands _____
         to accompany singers_____
         to rehearse_____

astronomy_ _to predict events_____
         to study the stars_____
         to study maps_____

biology_ _ _to study plants _____
         to study plants & animals_____
         to study animals _____

planets_ _ _within the country_____
         within our solar system _____
         within the Milky Way _____

LEVEL 10

draftsman_draws building plans _____
         draws pop designs _____
         works as a cartographer_____

chisel_ _ _ _chips wood or stone _____
         molds clay _____
         fastens studs _____

harmony_ _in discord_____
         in chords _____
         in dissonance _____

cello_ _ _ _in wind quartet _____
         in percussion quartet _____
         in string quartet _____

zoologist_ _studies animals_____
         studies circuses_____
         studies revivals_____

psychologist.at mental health clinics_____
         at orthopedic wards _____
         at obstetric wards _____

aquanaut_ _found in race boats _____
         found underwater_____
         found in the air _____

henna _ _ _ _to color hair red _____
         to feed to chickens _____
         to grow grass _____

Test 16   (cont.)

LEVEL 11

bears_____found hibernating in winter____   cupid_____found on valentines_____
found hibernating in summer__   found at Halloween_____
never hibernates_____   found in Cuba_____

papaya___to eat_____   oboe_____in a rock group_____
to drink_____   in an orchestra_____
to cook_____   in country music_____

astronomer observes and plots stars_____   professor___found in college_____
tells fortunes_____   found in hospitals_____
predicts events_____   found in libraries_____

plane_____to smooth paper_____   neurologist analyzes arteries_____
to smooth rough wood_____   studies behavior_____
to fasten plants_____   studies the nervous system____

Test 17   WORD RELATIONSHIPS

Description: This test is concerned with word analogies. (See pages 102-104.) Four examples are worked with the student initially to be sure that he understands words that are:

1. opposites
2. tied to characteristics
3. frequently associated
4. alternately tied, for example:

    cat is to dog AS meow is to _____
    bark

    In Item 4 the two words alternately tied are balanced by the *sound* typical of each animal. Alternately tied items are considered difficult.

Appropriate for: students high in decoding skills and low in comprehension. The test is also helpful for students who tend to CALL words in oral reading and who have difficulty comprehending in silent reading.

Ages: 7 through 14, or older students with learning difficulties

Testing Time: 10 minutes.

Directions for Use:
1. Administer the test individually or in small groups.
2. Do not use the test with students having less than second-grade reading ability.
3. Before presenting the test, work through the four examples that precede the test and be sure the student understands WHY the answers are correct.
4. If the student is in the primary grades, begin with the primary section (page 102); if intermediate, begin with the intermediate section (page 103); if upper, begin with the upper section (page 104).
5. If the student cannot answer 4 out of 6 correctly in the first set of the primary section, the test is too difficult and testing should be discontinued.

Scoring the Test: Answers to all test items are found on the "Answer Sheet and Record Form," page 101. Follow these guidelines in scoring.

1. The base level is 4 correct out of 6 items.
2. The failure level is 4 missed out of 6.

3. Mark a + for every correct response and a – for every incorrect one.
4. When in doubt, write the student's response to be scored at the completion of the test.
5. If at the end of the test the student scores lower than expected, the question remains as to whether he was unable to read the words or whether he read them and still didn't understand the relationship. In order to determine which is the case, the examiner should go through again and read the missed item aloud. The child's answer is then listed as an *aided* response.
6. Grading is as follows:

Grades	Expected Scores
2, 3	4-18
4, 5, 6	19-42
7, 8, 9	43-63

Remediation: Teach students to make up similar types of exercises to share with one another. Once a student understands word relationships to the extent that he can make up some of his own, he has a deeper understanding of them.

Practice Examples

"Read the words and try to select a word to fill in the final blank. Some words are opposites, some are characteristics, some words often go together and some words match alternately as in Item D."

If necessary, explain and work through the following examples with the student.

EXAMPLES:

A. girl -- boy AS woman -- _____

Ans. *man fellow guy* not brother or dad

Why: Because boy is the opposite of girl as man is the opposite of woman.

B. mosquitos -- fly AS ants -- _____

Ans. walk crawl run not dig

Why? Because flying is a characteristic mode of transportation for mosquitos just as walking, crawling or running is transportation for ants.

C. bread -- butter AS chair -- _____

Ans. *table*

Why? Because one word calls to mind the other in word associations.

D. cars -- lights AS gasoline -- _____

Ans. *electricity*

alternate balance
cars -- lights AS gasoline -- electricity

Why? Because these words are classed as a crossed or alternate relationship. Gasoline POWERS cars as electricity POWERS light.

Test 17   WORD RELATIONSHIPS   (Answer Sheet and Record Form)

Name _____ Grade _____   Chronological Age _____
yr.   mo.

Date of Test_____ Examiner _____

Observations:_____   Raw Score _____
_____   No. Attempted _____

O opposites   A word association
C characteristics of   * alternate relationships

ANSWERS

PRIMARY

O little/tiny/small/_____ 1
O lady/woman/ _____ 2
C climb/swing _____ 3
C chatter/squeal/ _____ 4
C trees/_____ 5
C chickens/hens/ _____ 6

C duck/ _____ 7
O down/ _____ 8
A glass/ _____ 9
C dog/pup/puppy/ _____ 10
O come/ _____ 11
C cat/ _____ 12

O happy/glad/ _____ 13
C eight/12/ _____ 14
A road/street/land _____ 15
A ring/ _____ 16
C plant/bush _____ 17
C black/ _____ 18

INTERMEDIATE

A hat/ _____ 19
C feet/ _____ 20
C ice/ _____ 21
A cars/motorcycles/trucks/ _____ 22
A men/ _____ 23
C 7/15 _____ 24

A kicking/_____ 25
C submerge/travel/underwater/float/ _____ 26
C build/saw/hammer _____ 27
* clay/silly putty/ _____ 28
* sing/ _____ 29
A drawing/sketching/ _____ 30

A wood/ _____ 31
C sew/ _____ 32
A feet/ _____ 33
A box _____ 34
O fall/ _____ 35
A moved out/vacated/ _____ 36

* ears/ _____ 37
C month/ _____ 38
A night/ _____ 39
C yellow/pink/ _____ 40
C yard/ _____ 41
C car/motorcycle/ _____ 42

UPPER

C fowl/birds/ _____ 43
* sailing/ _____ 44
A pine tree/ _____ 45
O backward/back up/fall back/ _____ 46
A bed/ _____ 47
C dry/hot _____ 48

C weeks/ _____ 49
* swimming/bathing/ _____ 50
A receiving/ _____ 51
* girls/ _____ 52
C songs/ _____ 53
C earth/land/ground/ _____ 54

C gallon/ _____ 55
A division/ _____ 56
C years/ _____ 57
O strong/ _____ 58
* spicy/ _____ 59
* vegetable/ _____ 60

* purple/violet/ _____ 61
* acting/ _____ 62
* acting/talking _____ 63

Give credit for ALL answers in the SAME relationship as the first of the equation. The most commonly given answers are listed here.

Test 17   WORD RELATIONSHIPS

PRIMARY

1. white — black AS big —————————————————
2. boy — girl AS man —————————————————
3. bird — fly AS monkey —————————————————
4. birds — sing AS monkeys —————————————————
5. raspberries — bushes AS apples —————————————
6. cub — bear AS chicks —————————————————

7. moo — cow AS quack —————————————————
8. hello — good-by AS up —————————————————
9. coffee — cup AS milk —————————————————
10. meow — cat AS bow-wow —————————————————
11. yes — no AS go —————————————————
12. puppy — dog AS kitty —————————————————

13. bad — good AS sad —————————————————
14. two — four AS six —————————————————
15. boat — water AS car —————————————————
16. wrist — watch AS finger —————————————————
17. plum — tree AS tomato —————————————————
18. pink — red AS gray —————————————————

Test 17 WORD RELATIONSHIPS (cont.)

INTERMEDIATE

19. feet — shoes AS head ————————————————
20. fingers — hand AS toes ————————————————
21. hot — water AS frozen ————————————————
22. house — people AS garage ————————————————
23. blouses — ladies AS shirts ————————————————
24. one — three AS five ————————————————

25. hands — catching AS feet ————————————————
26. 747 — fly AS submarines ————————————————
27. artists — draw AS carpenters ————————————————
28. paint — mold AS water colors ————————————————
29. dancers — singers AS dance ————————————————
30. brushes — painting AS pencils ————————————————

31. hammer — nails AS saw ————————————————
32. scissors — cut AS needles ————————————————
33. gloves — hand AS socks ————————————————
34. circle — ball AS square ————————————————
35. summer — winter AS spring ————————————————
36. bought — moved in AS sold ————————————————

37. see — hear AS eyes ————————————————
38. Monday — day AS January ————————————————
39. morning — day AS evening ————————————————
40. apple — red AS grapefruit ————————————————
41. inches — foot AS feet ————————————————
42. pedals — bicycle AS accelerator ————————————————

Test 17   WORD RELATIONSHIPS (cont.)

UPPER 7 — 9

43. skin — humans AS feathers ————————————————————————
44. rowboat — sailboat AS rowing ————————————————————
45. acorn — oaktree AS pine nut ————————————————————
46. advance — retreat AS forward ————————————————————
47. living room — davenport AS bedroom ——————————————
48. rain — wet AS sun ————————————————————————————

49. second — minutes AS days ————————————————————————
50. ice skate — bathing suit AS skating ——————————————
51. throwing — catching AS passing ——————————————————
52. trousers — skirt AS boys ——————————————————————
53. words — sentences AS notes ————————————————————
54. water — ocean AS soil ————————————————————————

55. cup — pint AS quart ————————————————————————————
56. addition — subtraction AS multiplication ——————————
57. weeks — months AS months ————————————————————
58. fragile — sturdy AS weak ——————————————————————
59. rice — chili AS bland ——————————————————————————
60. avocado — carrot AS fruit ————————————————————
61. yellow-red — blue-red AS orange ————————————————
62. dialogue — pantomine AS talking ——————————————————
63. opera — plays AS singing ————————————————————

Test 18   WORD SETS

Description: This is a test of words grouped in sets. (See page 109.) Students already dealing with sets in mathematics will understand the concept. Students not familiar with sets will have to have the concept explained to them.

The question that needs to be answered is: Why are these words grouped in this set? What meaning, range, or structural similarities do they have?

Appropriate for: students who have trouble with comprehension or who are considered "careless" readers.

Ages: 6 through 14, or older students with reading disabilities.

Testing Time: 10 minutes.

Directions for Use:
1. Administer the test individually or in small groups with students writing out their answers on the test form (page 109).
2. Work through the example given below and be sure that the student understands all possible answers.
3. Place the page of word sets in front of the student.
4. Start the student according to this chart, adjusting the difficulty up or down.

Grades	Word Sets
2 3	1
4 5 6	4
7 8 9	7

5. Direct the students as follows:
    "Give two reasons for these words to be grouped in sets." (If students are unfamiliar with the concept of sets, take some time to explain that words in sets have characteristics in common.)
    "Be sure that at least ONE of the reasons given tells something about the *meanings* of the words."

Example: Some of the reasons involving *meaning* are:

dog
cat
goldfish
horse
parrot

* They are all animals.
* They are all animated or alive — living things.
* They all eat.
* They could all be pets.
* They can move about.
* They are all found in the United States.
* They can all reproduce or have babies.

Some of the reasons involving *range* or *structure*:
* They ALL begin with a consonant.
* They are all English words with 8 letters or less.
* None of the words has more than 2 syllables.
* No word has less than 3 letters.
* All of the words have 2 or more consonants.
* All of the words have 1 or more vowels.

Scoring the Test: A selection of "Possible Answers" to the eight word sets begins on the bottom of this page and runs through page 108. Guidelines for scoring are as follows:

1. The student passes insofar as he or she is able to give two reasons for having the words belong to any particular set; however, one of the reasons MUST involve meaning.
2. The student earns bonus points for additional reasons. Bonus points DO NOT change the total raw score but are qualitatively considered.
3. Each answer involving meaning earns 2 points. Each answer involving range or structure earns 1 point.
4. The highest possible total raw score is 27 points, or 3 points per set.
5. In instances where the student gave several double or even ALL of the responses related to meaning these points may be added as bonus points and the student is given credit for stressing meaning:

Example: Student B earned a total of 27 points but for three of the sets he gave two responses and both related to meaning. This gives him a bonus score of 3 and the examiner records these responses as quality answers.

Remediation: Use the word index in the back of basal readers, social studies textbooks, and/or spellers as possible sources for additional word sets. After the words are arranged in sets, see how many characteristics the students can list to distinguish the words in each set.

When students can list the characteristics easily, ask them to prepare sets for their fellow students. To prepare original sets, the students need to use several reading skills — scanning, selecting, making judgments about word meaning, phonics, and structural relationships.

Possible Answers

go
come
play
work
sit
stand

Reasons with meaning — opposites in meaning
things people can do
action words — verbs
even little children can do these

range or structure — initial consonants
single syllables
English with 5 letters or less
no words less than 2 letters
have 1 or more vowels

big
large
tall
fat
huge
wide

meaning — expansive words
tells about dimensions
opposite of small, little,
short, skinny, tiny and
narrow
descriptive words
can describe a human
can describe inanimate things
non-living things

other — initial consonants
1 syllables
English words
none less than 3 letters
none more than 5 letters
all have 1 vowel or more

---

cars
trucks
vans
trains
trailors
mobiles

meaning — ground transportation
vehicles on wheels
driven by humans
powered by machines
driven by gas or diesel fuel

other — initial consonants
2 syllables or less
8 letters or less
English words
none less than 4 letters
1 vowel or more
plurals

---

lady
woman
female
she
gal
her

meaning — synonyms
all females
animate
living
may or may not be human

other — noun or pronouns
2 syllables or less
1 vowel or more
initial consonants

day night winter summer spring fall

meaning — opposites
    concerning time
    abstract words

other — initial consonants
    2 syllables or less
    6 letters or less
    3 letters or more
    1 vowel or more

---

airplanes gliders blimps helicopters dirigibles ballons

meaning — air transportation
    man guided
    launched at ground level
    landed at ground level

other — 4 syllables or less
    English words
    11 letters or less
    7 letters or more

---

explain exhale exchange exclaim exempt exert

meaning — differs in meaning
    all express action
    actions human can do

other — all begin with ex
    all have 2 syllables
    all have at least 2 vowels
    English words

---

pair pear plum plumb berry Barry

meaning — 3 sets of homonyms (homophones)
    1 in each pair is a fruit
    3 sets of words that sound alike but
      differ in meaning

other — initial consonants
    one or more vowels
    English
    4 or 5 letters
    2 syllables or less

---

odor smell scent odoriferous fragrance

meaning — synonyms
    sense of smell
    in human's awareness

other — 5 syllables or less
    English
    9 letters or less
    4 letters of more

Test 18   WORD SETS

Name _____ Grade _____   Chronological Age_____
                                                              yr.   mo.
Date of Test _____ Examiner _____   Meaningful Ans. _____
Observations:_____   Other Ans. _____
_____   TOTAL_____
_____   Bonus Points _____

go
come
play
work
sit
stand
1__

M _____
O _____
+ _____

big
large
tall
fat
huge
wide
2__

M _____
O _____
+ _____

cars
trucks
vans
trains
trailors
mobiles
3__

M _____
O _____
+ _____

lady
woman
female
she
gal
her
4__

M _____
O _____
+ _____

day
night
winter
summer
spring
fall
5__

M _____
O _____
+ _____

blimps
airplanes
gliders
helicopters
dirigibles
balloons
6__

M _____
O _____
+ _____

explain
exhale
exchange
exempt
exert
7__

M _____
O _____
+ _____

pair
pear
plum
berry
Barry
8__

M _____
O _____
+ _____

odor
smell
scent
odoriferous
fragrance
9__

M _____
O _____
+ _____

Section IV Summary

Section IV contains two forms of a graded word list: San Diego Quick Assessment, Form I and Form II. These tests are suggested as entry tests leading directly to instruction, and to additional tests as warranted.

Tests 13 and 14 sample students' skills in applied phonics and structural analysis.

All other tests in this section deal with words at the semantic level: Test 15 as antonyms; Test 16 as definitions; Test 17 as analogies, and Test 18 is a general review.

Tests in this section cover decoding and structure, sight words, word opposites, word uses or locations, word relationships and word sets. Most of the tests relate to immediate recognition of words and to UNDERSTANDING words as they relate to other words.

References

Barnell Loft, Ltd., Rockville Center, New York.

Harris, Albert J. and Edward R. Sipay. *How to Increase Readability,* 6th ed. New York: David McKay, Inc., 1975.

Hayakawa, Samuel I. *Language in Thought and Action,* 2nd ed. New York: Harcourt Brace Jovanovich, 1964.

Heilman, Arthur W. *Phonics in Proper Perspective,* 3rd ed. Columbus, Ohio: Merrill, 1976.

_____, and Elizabeth Ann Holmes. *Smuggling Language into the Teaching of Reading.* Columbus, Ohio: Merrill, 1972.

Kottmeyer, William. *Basic Goals in Spelling.* New York: McGraw-Hill, 1972.

LaPray, Margaret H. *Teaching Children to Become Independent Readers.* West Nyack, N.Y.: The Center for Applied Research in Education, Inc., 1972.

Miller, Wilma H. *Structural Analysis Activity Sheets,* Unit IV in the "Corrective Reading Skills Activity File." West Nyack, N.Y.: The Center for Applied Research in Education, Inc., 1977.

Smith, E. Brooks, Kenneth Goodman, and Robert Meredith, *Language and Thinking in the Elementary School.* New York: Holt, Rinehart & Winston, 1970.

Thorndike, E.L. *Thorndike-Century Junior Dictionary.* New York: Scott, Foresman.

Washington, E.D., and J.A. Tesks, "Relations between the Wide Range Achievement Test and the California Achievement Test, the Stanford Binet and the Illinois Test of Psycholinguistic Abilities," *Psychological Reports,* Vol. 26, No. 1 (1970), 291-94.

Zintz, Miles V. *Corrective Reading,* 3rd ed. Dubuque, Iowa: Wm. C. Brown, 1977.

SECTION V

measuring skills with phrases

(Contains Tests 19 through 24)

Soon after the student begins to read, at whatever rudimentary level, he or she needs to realize the importance of grouping words into phrases. In this section, phrases are identified as any 2 to 6 words that sound better combined than separated. Tests in this section cover prepositions, nouns, and verb phrases. Even before students are aware of these classifications, they should be able to group words together because they are so grouped in daily conversation.

Some students persist in reading word by word and need additional help in learning to phrase. Tests in this section are designed to pinpoint weaknesses in identifying phrases. Furthermore, the tests distinguish between identifying words as part of a phrase and the phrase itself.

Table VI provides a brief overview of the tests.

Table VI
Test Guide 19-24

Test	Title	Ages	Minutes	Appropriate for students who:
19	Phrase Levels	7-14	5	have low comprehension scores and phrase incorrectly
20	Prepositions	7-9	3	tend to read word by word and read prepositions as separate from phrases
21	Listening Aural-Visual and Encoding	7-10	5	tend to read words correctly but have difficulty in understanding what they read
22	Noun Phrases	7-10	8	tend to "call words"
23	Verb Phrases	7-9	8	tend to "call words" and separate parts of predicates
24	Identifying Phrases	7-10	8	tend to read word by word or incorrectly group words

Test 19   PHRASE LEVELS

Description: This test is a measure of the student's understanding of prepositional phrases. It contains 36 phrases to be matched with other phrases similar or close in meaning. (See pages 114-115.)

Appropriate for: students who tend to have low comprehension scores, who read word by word, and who are unable to phrase correctly in oral reading.

Ages: 7 through 14, and older students with reading disabilities.

Testing Time: 5 minutes.

Directions for Use:
1. Administer the test to the class or to individuals.
2. Use Part I with average second, third, and fourth graders.
   Use Part II with average fifth, sixth, and seventh graders.
   Use Part III with average eighth- and ninth-grade students.
3. Try to reach a basal of 3 consecutive passes.
4. Stop testing with 3 consecutive errors.

Scoring the Test: See the "Answer Key" for the test below. Scoring is as follows:
1. Score 1 point for each phrase correctly underlined.
2. Stop testing at 3 consecutive failures.

Grade Levels	Expected Range of Scores
2, 3, 4	3-14
5, 6, 7	12-26
8, 9	24-36

Remediation: Have students underline prepositional phrases from sources such as old, used workpages and explain the meaning of these phrases in their own words.

Example: | for her grandmother | "This is a present that someone wrapped to give to grandmother."

Answer Key

I.

1. a place to walk
2. a place to read
3. for birds to fly
4. a place to play
5. a place to climb
6. for dogs to sleep

7. to house cows
8. a place to fish
9. thick frosting
10. her chair
11. green grass
12. lots of sailboats

II.

13. are picnic grounds
14. dining room rug
15. is immediate
16. some poems
17. the ocean floor
18. some unusual cacti

19. red geraniums
20. pastel sweet peas
21. a yardstick
22. really old movies
23. possible floods
24. lighted planes

III.

25. mostly mortar
26. trash bins
27. pans are stored
28. some men suffered
29. black coal
30. to view art objects

31. are valuable things
32. are weeds
33. are barnacles
34. houses toppled
35. the sun is overhead
36. is one year

Test 19   PHRASE LEVELS

Name _____ Grade _____ Chronological Age _____

Date _____ Examiner _____

Observations: _____

_____

	yr.	mo.
I Primary	_____	out of 12
II Intermediate	_____	out of 12
III Secondary	_____	out of 12

Underline the phrase that goes BEST with the phrase already underlined.

I.

1. down the stairs
   a place to swim
   a place to walk
   a place to somersault

2. inside of school
   a place to bathe
   a place to scream
   a place to read

3. up in the sky
   for birds to fly
   for birds to swim
   for ants to build

4. out in the yard
   a place to undress
   a place to sleep
   a place to play

5. over the fence
   a place to lie down
   a place to climb
   a place to bicycle

6. under the steps
   for dogs to sleep
   for fish to swim
   for giraffes to eat

7. in the barn
   to house people
   to house cows
   to house monkeys

8. beside the river
   a place for cars
   a place for tractors
   a place to fish

9. on top of the cake
   thick frosting
   thin frostbite
   for freezing

10. near teacher's desk
    her house
    her chair
    her auto

11. beneath the trees
    green grass
    round cookies
    warm soup

12. close to the ocean
    lots of sailboats
    wide deserts
    French bakeries

II.

13. beside a brook
    are car salesman
    are picnic grounds
    are theaters

14. underneath a table
    table cloths
    wall paper
    dining room rug

15. at once
    is immediate
    is eminent
    is unnecessary

16. in a book of verse
    some plays
    some poems
    mostly prose

Test 19 (cont.)

17. below sea level
    the ocean floor
    the mountain top
    the Indian Ocean

18. in the desert
    some salt water taffy
    some unusual cacti
    some artesian springs

19. for house plants
    red geraniums
    tall oak trees
    black and white koalas

20. beside a garden wall
    pastel sweet peas
    sweeping brooms
    steaming sweet rolls

21. three feet long
    a centimeter
    a ruler
    a yard stick

22. on the late show
    really old movies
    really new movies
    really silly cartoons

23. at sea level
    never floods
    possible floods
    baked dry

24. in the night sky
    lighted trucks
    unlighted planes
    lighted planes

III.

25. between the wall bricks
    mostly mortar
    mostly sand
    mostly water

26. behind the restaurant
    tractor piles
    trash bins
    Christmas packages

27. beside the stove
    straw is kept
    fish are stored
    pans are stored

28. after the war
    some men suffered
    zoos were closed
    women were deported

29. beneath the ground
    gold bracelets
    black coal
    red tomatoes

30. to the museum
    to view art objects
    to trade stories
    to check out books

31. under lock and key
    are the inflammables
    are valuable things
    are valueless jewels

32. in between the grass blades
    are weeds
    are wenches
    are cellos

33. underneath the bottom of the boat
    are oars
    are fishing seats
    are barnacles

34. by a hurricane
    houses toppled
    children slept
    teachers taught swimming

35. about 12 noon each day
    the sun is in the east
    the sun is overhead
    the sun is in the west

36. from January through December
    is one year
    is one month
    is one week

Test 20 PREPOSITIONS

Description: In this test the student is to identify 21 prepositions. (See pages 118-119.) Prepositions in items 1 through 21 and phrases in items 22 through 27 are read aloud by the student. Phrases 28 through 39 are read silently and are matched to the correct picture.

Appropriate for: students who did poorly on Test 19, who read orally word by word, and who have poor comprehension.

Ages: 7 through 9 and older students having reading disabilities.

Testing Time: 3 minutes.

Directions for Use:
> Part I is to be administered individually.
> Part II can be administered to the class. "Draw a line from the phrase to the picture that matches the phrase."

Scoring the Test: Students who are able to read 20 of the 27 prepositions and phrases in Part I may complete Part II of the test on their own. Those who identify 19 or less should be taught the remainder before proceeding to Part II.

Remediation: Students who identify 19 or less of the prepositions on Part I should have the missed prepositions placed on matching cards:
> 1. Time the student in matching the sets.
> 2. Read each of the sets ALOUD.
> 3. Use the sets on a concentration board.

Students who score 9 or less out of 12 on Part II should be given activity cards that require them to follow directions:

> Materials: 1 ball, 1 box, 1 set of activity cards:
> > Put the ball —

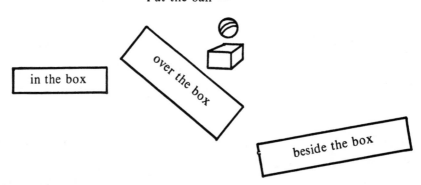

Another effective remedial technique is to ask some students to copy sentences omitting the prepositions and ask another student to fill in the blanks. Students who fill in the blanks can check the original source of the sentences to see how many prepositions match the originals.

Have one student copy 6 short sentences all with 1 key preposition omitted. On the following day have the same student see if he is able to fill in all of the blanks to make plausible reading.

Sample set of 6 sentences:

for	"This present is _____ you," he said.
from	"It is _____ me."
with	"I bought it _____ my money."
by	"I earned this money _____ working."
under	"The present is _____ the Christmas tree."

Test 20   PREPOSITIONS

Name _____ Grade _____   Chronological Age _____
                                                                    yr.   mo.
Date _____ Examiner_____   Oral _____ out of _____
Observations: _____   Comprehension _____ out of _
_____
_____

PART I

A. "Read as many of these words aloud as you can."

1. in	8. with	15. into
2. on	9. above	16. with
3. from	10. of	17. over
4. under	11. at	18. before
5. to	12. below	19. along
6. for	13. near	20. between
7. beside	14. after	21. by

B. "Read as many of these phrases as you can."

22. in the box	25. above the box
23. from the box	26. near the box
24. under the box	27. between the boxes

Test 20 (cont.)

PART II

"Draw a line from the phrase to the picture that matches the phrase."

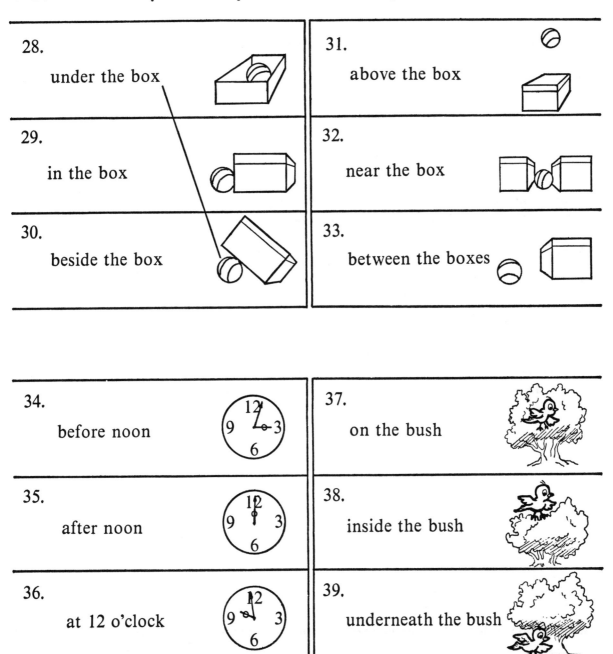

28. under the box

29. in the box

30. beside the box

31. above the box

32. near the box

33. between the boxes

34. before noon

35. after noon

36. at 12 o'clock

37. on the bush

38. inside the bush

39. underneath the bush

Test 21   LISTENING AURAL-VISUAL and ENCODING

Description: In this test students listen to paragraphs that are read or taped by the teacher as they follow along on a printed form (see pages 122-123). After the teacher says, "Mark," the students write in prepositions. The tasks are fourfold:

1. Words heard must be correctly *matched* to the visual symbols.
2. Prepositions to be filled in the blank space must be *held in short-term memory.*
3. These words must then be *encoded* (written) in the correct blanks.
4. These prepositions must be written in the *correct sound-sequence* and, therefore, MAY be phonetically spelled.

Appropriate for: students who tend to miscall small words, whose comprehension is low, and who have difficulty recognizing prepositional phrases.

Ages: 7 through 10, or older students with reading disabilities.

Testing Time: 5 minutes.

Directions for Use:

To prepare for the test, duplicate the test form (pages 122-123) as a student's copy. Duplicate another form with the answers copied in as the teacher's form. The answers are given in the "Answer Key" following this test information.

1. Administer the test to individuals or in small groups.
2. Remind the student to "listen carefully" before each paragraph is read aloud.
3. Begin testing:

Ages	Paragraphs
7 yrs. — 9.0 yrs.	1 through 5
9.1 yrs. — 10 yrs.	6 through 10

Scoring the Test: There are 41 items to be scored. A base score is achieved when ALL of the prepositions are correctly filled in for one paragraph. All paragraphs below this level are given full credit.

The ceiling is reached when 3 or more items are missed in one paragraph.

Since this is NOT a spelling test, any phonetic spelling of the prepositions is acceptable, such as *beecide* in place of *beside,* and even *four* in place of *for.*

Remediation: Students who cannot complete half of the items in this test need to be given intensive practice in similar types of exercises. There are many sources of phrase drills, such as Dolch's

Picture Phrases and others. Effective teacher-made material can be prepared from prepositional phrases picked up from old workbooks.

Answer Key

(Answers to be written in teacher's copy.)

1. in, to, after
2. in, In, for, over
3. to, on, on, from
4. in, from, of, with
5. in, through, After, over

6. with, from, into, against, of
7. into, inside, with, without, to
8. over, Of, without, through
9. of, at, beside, at
10. about, with, as, to, behind

Test 21   LISTENING AURAL-VISUAL and ENCODING

Name _____ Grade _____   Chronological Age _____

<table>
<tr><td></td><td></td><td>yr.</td><td>mo.</td></tr>
<tr><td>Date _____ Examiner _____</td><td>Primary 1-5 _____</td><td></td><td>/19</td></tr>
<tr><td>Observations:_____</td><td>Intermed. 6-10 _____</td><td></td><td>/22</td></tr>
<tr><td>_____</td><td>Total _____</td><td>out of 41</td><td></td></tr>
</table>

"Listen carefully as I read these sentences and paragraphs. When I stop reading, see if you can write in the words that I said to fill in the blanks. Do not write until I say, *"Mark."*"

1. Fish can swim _____ the water.
    Birds have wings _____ fly.
    Cats run _____ mice

2. I swim _____ summer. _____ winter I think the ocean is too cold _____ swimming. So we have a boat and we ride all _____ the bay.

3. I go _____ school _____ Monday, Tuesday, Wednesday, Thursday, and Friday. But I can play _____ Saturday and Sunday _____ one to four in the afternoon.

4. Spiders spin webs _____ the corners. They spin webs _____ the ceiling and out _____ the way places. The web is spun tight _____ close threads to catch little bugs.

5. Bears hibernate _____ winter. They eat enough to last them _____ the cold winter months. _____ they dig in, the heavy snows fall _____ their dens.

6. The earth is covered _____ our atmosphere. This atmosphere is like a protective blanket that shades off the extreme heat _____ the sun. Astronauts who travel out _____ the atmosphere must be well insulated _____ the rays _____ the sun.

7. Aquanauts dive _____ the water. They study underwater sea life _____ diving bells or _____ scuba diving equipment and nets. Often they appear to be _____ fear even when sharks swim _____ them.

Test 21   (cont.)

8. There are many vehicles that can fly _____ head. The most common of these is the airplane, but there are blimps, dirigibles, and airborne balloons. _____ most interest, however, are the airborne persons _____ motors such as glider pilots and man-carrying kites. These persons glide _____ the air in a miraculous way.

9. Africa has many animals, most _____ which you have already seen _____ the zoo. Not all zoos have an okapi, however. This animal resembles a giraffe, though it is smaller, is unspotted, and has a shorter neck. Actually the okapi looks dwarfed _____ the giraffe. But even a glance _____ the two will tell the zoo visitor that these herbivorous animals are related.

10. Read this and you may learn something new _____ the woodchuck. A woodchuck is a burrowing rodent _____ a thick body and short tail, but it is also classed _____ a marmot. Marmots are indigenous _____ North America, Europe and Asia. Actually you may see a woodchuck _____ a tree on your next walk in the woods.

Test 22   NOUN PHRASES

Description: This test has two parts. (See page 125.) Part I consists of 14 noun determiners such as *a, the, my, his,* and 14 frequently used adjectives. A rebus is used in place of each noun. Students are expected to read this part aloud.

In Part II, students are expected to read the noun phrases silently and to match them by writing the number of the phrase just read aloud that means nearly the same. The first phrase is worked as an example.

Appropriate for: students who tend to read word by word, whose comprehension is poor, and who have difficulty recognizing phrases.

Ages: 7 through 10, and older students who have reading disabilities.

Testing Time: 8 minutes.

Directions for Use:
Administer Part I individually.
Administer Part II to the whole class or in small groups.

Scoring the Test: Part I if totally correct is equal to 14 points. However, it is important to note the speed of the student's response, the correct intonation and confidence of response.

Part II totals 13 points, and the correct answers are provided below. The speed of response should also be noted.

Remediation: Use pages from old worksheets, magazines, and even obsolete books. For students who made errors in Part I, it is valuable to have them underline all of the determiners at the beginning of sentences, and also to have them underline descriptive words or adjectives preceding nouns. Finally, students should underline the total noun phrases and read these aloud to another student.

If there are any students who continue to read word by word, provide an oral model for the student to "echo back," or use a neurological impress method described by Heckleman (see the reference at the end of the section). Another good technique is to have the teacher and student read the phrase *TOGETHER once* and immediately after this have the student read the phrase independently.

Answers to Part II

(2)	14
1	13
3	8
7	12
6	10
5	11
4	9

Test 22   NOUN PHRASES

I. Read the following phrase aloud.

1   a tall

2   a plump

3   this old-fashioned

4   that red

5   those orange

6   these round

7   my pretty

8   his old

9   her broad

10   some fat

11   nine beautiful

12   one lonesome

13   a few delicious

14   their expensive

II. Fill in the number of the phrase from those above that best matches these phrases in meaning.

__2__ a plump hen

_____ a tall skyscraper

_____ this old-styled hat

_____ my pretty dress

_____ these red apples

_____ those orange ribbons

_____ that red fox

_____ their expensive car

_____ a few delicious candies

_____ his old beard

_____ one lonesome boy

_____ some plump pigs

_____ nine lovely candles

_____ her wide forehead

Test 23   VERB PHRASES

Description: This test has two parts. (See page 127.) Part I consists of 14 verbs, auxiliary verbs, infinitives, and adverbs to be read aloud by the student. This part of the test measures the student's automatic response to verb phrases.

In Part II, 12 verb phrases are read silently and matched with the correct picture.

Appropriate for: students who tend to read word by word, who score poorly in comprehension, and who phrase incorrectly.

Ages: 7 through 9 and older students who have reading disabilities.

Testing Time: 8 minutes.

Directions for Use:
Administer Part I individually.
Part II may be administered to the whole class or to small groups.

Scoring the Test: Part I if totally correct is equal to 14 points. Note the speed of response, the correct intonation, and the confidence of the student's response.

Part II totals 12 points and the speed of response should also be noted.

Remediation: Collect sheets rich in verb phrases from such sources as old worksheets and magazines. Students who score low in Part I should have a chance to practice by listening to a model read the phrases, underlining them, and then, in turn, echoing them back.

Students low in Part II should be given a chance to mark the verb phrases in old worksheets. They should then explain their actions in their own words.

Test 23   VERB PHRASES

Name _____ Grade _____   Chronological Age_____

                                                                                   yr.   mo.

Date_____ Examiner_____   Part I _____ out of 14 points

Observations:_____   Part II _____ out of 12 points

_____   Total _____ out of 26 points

I. Read the following phrases aloud.

1. are running	8. is close
2. likes to eat	9. loves to skip
3. was falling	10. came slowly
4. am winning	11. has turned around
5. were fighting	12. have already gone
6. went fishing	13. weren't playing
7. can jump up	14. can't skate

II. Match the following phrases to the pictures.

living here•

falling down •

rowing out •

is catching•

were fighting•

are swimming•

turning somersaults•

are jumping•

was eating •

loves to paint •

can bat •

went skating•

Test 24   IDENTIFYING PHRASES

Description: This is a listening exercise in which students hear phrases and are expected to put slash lines marking the reader's phrasing on their test forms. (See pages 130-131.)

Appropriate for: students who tend to read in a monotone, who read one word at a time, who are non-fluent and/or who have poor comprehension.

Ages: 7 through 9, and older students with reading disabilities.

Testing Time: 8 minutes.

Directions for Use:

To prepare for the test, the teacher should mark a copy of the test form as shown on page 129 in "Teacher's Copy."

1. Administer the test individually or in small groups.
2. Before reading each paragraph, remind students to "listen carefully."
3. Be sure students have finished marking before proceeding to the next paragraph.
4. As you work through the example, make a judgment about the student's competence. If working the example was difficult, continue with paragraph 1. If working through the example seemed easy, start with a more difficult paragraph.

Scoring the Test: There are 93 slash marks possible. These slash lines should be uniformly marked as the teacher/reader makes obvious, though not too exaggerated, pauses at these points.

Each paragraph is passed if no more than one slash mark is omitted. Testing should be stopped with the paragraph in which 4 or more of the slash marks are incorrect.

Remediation: Extended testing may be used as part of the remediation in this test of phrasing. Another suggestion is to determine, on an individual basis, how quickly the student "catches on" to the slash marks. After the student has correctly marked (with help, if necessary) two paragraphs that were incorrectly marked at the first testing, ask him/her to read them aloud with appropriate pauses where slash marks occur.

Pair students and have one read aloud while the other student marks phrases on old worksheets or workbook pages.

To assist the teacher in marking his/her own copy, place slash marks in the example as follows:

Some fish/are fat./ Some fish/are skinny./
Some fish/are pretty,/and some fish/are not./

For uniformity in administering the remainder of the test, place slash marks by counting the words as follows:

Paragraph 1:	2/2./2/2./2/3,/2/2./	(8)
Paragraph 2:	2/2./2/2./2/3/3/2./	(16)
Paragraph 3:	2/3./2/3/2./3/3/2/3./4/2./	(27)
Paragraph 4:	2/2/2./5/4/4./3/4./3/3/2/5/2./	(40)
Paragraph 5:	3/2/2./3/2/4./4/3./3/2,/4/3./	(52)
Paragraph 6:	3/4/3/3/4/2,/4/4/2./3/3,/3/5,/3/2./	(67)
Paragraph 7:	3/3/4./2,/4/3./4/5,/3/2/3/3./	(79)
Paragraph 8:	2/2/3./2/4/6/5./6/4/3/4./5/5/3./	(93)

Test 24 IDENTIFYING PHRASES

Name _____ Grade _____ Chronological Age_____

                                                                              yr.   mo.

Date _____ Examiner _____ No. Correct _____ out of ___

Observations:_____

Make a slash / mark whenever you hear a break between groups of words:
Example: Some fish/ are fat./ Some fish/ are skinny./
                  Some fish/ are pretty,/ and some fish/ are not./

1. Some houses are tall. Some houses are small.
Some houses are brightly painted, and some are not.

2. Some cars are new. Some cars are old.
Some cars are painted blue but some cars are not.

3. Some zoos have exotic birds. Some zoos have no birds at all. San Diego Zoo has both birds and animals of all sizes. The San Diego Zoo is famous.

4. Koala bears are found in Australia. However, they are also present in the San Diego and the Chicago Zoos. Koalas are natives of the down-under country. United States zoos try to provide an environment as much like their home as possible.

5. The Wright brothers were intelligent and ambitious. As young men they ran a bicycle repair shop. Their mother encouraged them in their efforts. They were creative and inventive, and she was proud of their talent.

6. Producing a play is an exciting venture but don't plan to try it unless you have nerves of steel, the patience of Job and an endless will to succeed. If you possess all these attributes, plus a cast with at least moderate talent, your production worries are over.

Test 24   (cont.)

7. Leonardo de Vinci was an artist all of his life. What's more, he was an inventor and a genius. Long before the airplane was in its experimental stages, Leonardo sketched planes that indicated a correct understanding of airflow principles.

8. The earth is covered with an atmosphere. This atmosphere is like a blanket that shades off the extreme heat of the sun's direct rays. Astronauts who travel through this atmosphere and into the stratosphere need protective insulation against such heat rays. Both the capsule carrying them and their own space suits are well insulated.

Section V Summary

All of the tests in this section are appropriate for word-by-word readers and/or students who group words incorrectly.

Test 19 assesses the *understanding* of prepositional phrases for elementary through junior high school levels. Part I of Test 20 is used to discover if the high frequency preposition words are known as sight words and also as a part of a phrase. Part II of this test assesses an understanding of prepositional phrases by matching the phrase to the correct picture.

Test 21 measures the student's ability to:

1. Listen and follow as sentences and paragraphs are read aloud.
2. Retain in "short term memory" prepositions read orally.
3. Encode prepositions previously read to students who will then fill in the blank spaces.

Test 22 assesses fluency and understanding of noun phrases. Part I tests fluency whereas Part II tests the student's ability to read the written noun in place of the rebus.

Test 23, Part I, measures the student's oral fluency in reading verb phrases. Part II of this test measures the student's understanding of verb phrases.

Test 24 is a test of the student's ability to hear all types of phrases, and to follow along and mark these phrases on a typed copy.

References

Durell, Donald D. *Improving Reading Instruction.* New York: Harcourt Brace Jovanovich, 1956.

Heckleman, R.G., "Using the Neurological Impress Remedial Technique," *Academic Therapy Quarterly,* 1966, 235-239.

Levin, Harry, and Eleanor L. Kaplan, "Grammatical Structure and Reading," in Harry Levin and Joanna P. Williams (eds.) *Basic Studies in Reading.* New York: Basic Books, 1970, pp. 119-133.

SECTION VI

measuring sentence skills

(Contains tests 25 through 31)

Students may comprehend word boundaries, word relationships, phrases, and yet have difficulty comprehending at the sentence level. Additional constraints are placed on words as they appear in sentences and all of the tests in this section are designed to measure sensitivity to these constraints. Comprehension is measured in a variety of ways: by matching sentences close in meaning but reworded, by a cloze procedure, by unscrambling jumbled sentences, and by interpreting idiomatic expressions.

The following Test Guide (Table VII) provides an overview of the tests for measuring students' skills with sentences.

Table VII
Test Guide 25-31

Test	Title	Ages	Minutes	Appropriate for students who:
25	Sentences Reworded	6-16	8	comprehend words and phrases but fail at some point beyond
26	Context Clues	6-13	10	score low on Test 25
27	Nouns Out	6.6-13	10	score low on either Test 25 or Test 26
28	Verbs Out	6.6-13	10	score low on Tests 25, 26 and/or 27
29	Adjectives Out	6.6-14	10	score low on Tests 25, 26 27 and/or 28
30	Jumbled Sentences	6.6-16	10	score low on Test 25
31	Cultural Sampling	11-16	8	enter with a foreign background or from a subculture

Test 25   SENTENCES REWORDED

Description: This test consists of two parts. (See pages 136-137.) Part I involves 15 sentences in five units of three, which have to be matched with 15 sentences in five units of three, which have been reworded.

Part II involves 30 sentences in six units of five which have to be matched with 30 sentences in six units of five, which have been reworded.

Appropriate for: students who have mastered comprehension at the word and phrase level, but who have difficulty understanding meaning at the sentence level.

Ages: 6 to 16, and older students with reading disabilities.

Testing Time: 8 minutes.

Directions for Use:
1. Administer the test to small groups or to the total class.
2. Be sure the three sentences in the example are marked correctly.
3. Begin at a point at which a student can read all the sentences in one group correctly.

Scoring the Test: Answers to both parts of the test are provided in the following Answer Key.

Basal Level is that group of sentences in which the student matches ALL of the sentences correctly. Students are then given credit for all of the sentences BELOW this level.

Ceiling level is reached at the point where two consecutive units are incorrectly matched. An incorrect unit is defined as a group of five sentences in which three or more are incorrectly matched.

Grade Placement	Expected Scores
Grade 1	3-6
Grade 2	7-9
Grade 3	10-12
Grade 4	13-15
Grade 5	16-20
Grade 6	21-25
Grade 7	26-30
Grade 8	31-35
Grade 9	36-40
Grade 10	41-45

Remediation: Children of at least average intelligence (an IQ of 90 or above) who score 4 or more points below the expected score for their grade should be assigned a remedial program which stresses comprehension at the sentence level. There are many commercially available programs which do this, including those published by Dexter and Westbrook Ltd. and Reader's Digest

Workshop I and II. If such programs are not available to the teacher, items similar to those found on the test itself can be made up.

Example: Student A in grade 10, of average intelligence, scores 37, or 4 points below the expected range of 41-45. Student A's program of remediation needs to include attention to comprehension at the sentence level.

Answer Key

Part I

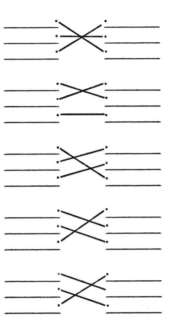

___

Part II

5. $\dfrac{5}{3}$ ...
    $\dfrac{}{2}$
    $\dfrac{}{4}$
    $\dfrac{}{1}$

8. $\dfrac{17}{20}$
    $\dfrac{}{19}$
    $\dfrac{}{16}$
    $\dfrac{}{18}$

6. $\dfrac{6}{10}$
    $\dfrac{}{7}$
    $\dfrac{}{8}$
    $\dfrac{}{9}$

9. $\dfrac{24}{21}$
    $\dfrac{}{25}$
    $\dfrac{}{22}$
    $\dfrac{}{23}$

7. $\dfrac{15}{14}$
    $\dfrac{}{11}$
    $\dfrac{}{13}$
    $\dfrac{}{12}$

10. $\dfrac{30}{26}$
    $\dfrac{}{28}$
    $\dfrac{}{29}$
    $\dfrac{}{27}$

Test 25   SENTENCES REWORDED

Name _____ Grade _____   Chronological Age _____

Date _____ Examiner _____   yr.   mo.

Observations: _____   Starting Level _____

_____   Total Score _____

_____

PART I.   "There is more than *one* way to say most things. Draw a line from the sentence on the left to the one on the right that is reworded."

Example: You come here.   • Jump up.
        Please jump up.   • Were you right?
        Did you do it right?   • Come here.

This is my cat.   • He likes to bat.
I can jump.   • See me jump.
He likes baseball.   • See my cat.

Can I go with you?   • I want to stay.
Please let me stay here.   • Please take me too.
I've got many good friends.   • I have lots of friends.

Jack jump over the candlestick   • Something sat by her.
The spider sat beside her.   • She moved fast.
She jumped up quickly.   • Jump over this.

Little Jack Horner sat in a corner.   • I am a good boy.
He pulled out a plum.   • Jack sat alone.
And said, "What a good boy am I."   • He found a plum.

Fern began to cry.   • Don't kill the runt.
She felt sorry for the runt.   • Fern cried.
She told her dad to spare the runt.   • Fern was sad.

PART II.   "Fill in the number of the sentence which means nearly the same as the sentence on the left side of the page."

Amelia Bedelia tried to do exactly as she was told and that got her into all kinds of trouble:

_____ She dressed the chicken.
_____ She filed papers.
_____ She drew the curtains.
_____ She trimmed the meat.
_____ She dusted the furniture.

1. She put dusting powder on the table and chairs.

2. She took crayons and made a picture of the curtains.

3. She took a wood file to scrape the papers.

4. She decorated the steak with bows and ribbons.

5. She put clothes on the chicken.

Test 25 (cont.)

Homer's uncle forgot to tell him how to turn off the doughnut machine.

_____ Homer couldn't figure out how to turn off the machine.
_____ A wealthy woman offered to mix the doughnut dough.
_____ She lost her valuable diamond ring in the batter.
_____ We'll offer a reward for my ring.
_____ The doughnuts sold like hotcakes.

6. He couldn't stop the machine.
7. My ring is in a doughnut.
8. There's money for whoever finds my ring.
9. The doughnuts went fast.
10. "Let me mix the batter."

Karana was left for 18 years to live on the Island of the Blue Dolphins.

_____ Karana lived a lonely life.
_____ Karana faced many dangers daily.
_____ She no longer wanted to "get even."
_____ She was self-sufficient.
_____ She was finally brought from the bleak island to civilization.

11. She lost her need for revenge.
12. She was rescued.
13. She took care of herself.
14. Every day was filled with danger.
15. "It's lonely here."

Breathin' Man was an unusual person.

_____ Breathin' Man was a resourceful person.
_____ He had a habit of dozing off.
_____ He was amazingly thoughtful of others.
_____ He inherited a small fortune.
_____ He could often arrange for things to happen.

16. He inherited wealth.
17. Breathin' Man found what he wanted.
18. He worked to bring about certain events.
19. He was considerate.
20. He took naps often.

Willie Wonka's factory made chocolate bars.

_____ Willie Wonka ran a chocolate factory.
_____ He sponsored a contest.
_____ He was a most unusual man.
_____ He hired many workers.
_____ He didn't know that Charlie Bucket would be one of the winners.

21. Willie Wonka promised prizes.
22. He had a large labor force.
23. He had no idea who would win a prize.
24. He managed a large chocolate factory.
25. He was different from most men.

Tom didn't always obey, he didn't like work or school but he did like Becky.

_____ Tom was sly and usually got away without doing his share.
_____ Tom and Becky found themselves in a dangerous situation.
_____ Aunt Polly often lost her patience with Tom.
_____ Tom didn't return home and no one knew where he was.
_____ Tom and Becky were fond of one another.

26. They got into difficulty.
27. They liked each other.
28. She was impatient with Tom.
29. He ran away.
30. He avoided working whenever possible.

137

Test 26   CONTEXT CLUES

Description: This test consists of 40 sentences with five types of clues given following letter designations from A to E. (See pages 140-143.) The test is designed to focus on the types of context clues that the student uses well and to discover the types he/she has not yet learned to make use of.

Appropriate for: students who tend to miscall words, who are non-fluent readers, and who have low rates of comprehension.

Ages: 6 to 16.

Testing Time: 10 minutes.

Directions for Use:
1. Administer the test in small groups or to the whole class.
2. Be sure that the examples are correctly marked.
3. If possible, begin at the part where the student can mark all five from A to E correctly.

Scoring: See the following key for answers to each of the eight sets of sentences in the test. Basal Level is the highest group of A through E that is all correctly marked. The ceiling is any group of A through E in which two or more sentences are marked incorrectly.

Grade Placement	*Expected Scores*
1	3-5
2	6-8
3	9-11
4	12-14
5	15-17
6	18-20
7	21-23
8	24-29
9	30-35
10	36-40

Remediation: Make up activities similar to those found in this test. Practice with all types of cloze exercises. Cloze activities are those in which every 5th, 7th, or 10th word (except proper nouns) has been deleted.

Another guide for use in remediation is found in the pattern of blanks to be filled in by the student:

A. word already used
B. word defined
C. synonym given
D. antonym given
E. from experience, vicarious or real

If the student misses more of one type of context clues than another, exercises can be designed to fit that particular type.

In extended testing teach the items missed and retest on the following day.

Answer Key

I. another, hopped, unhappy, gate, snow
II. along, fruit, quick, teach, ticking
III. cheek, reason, plain, freeze, knife
IV. Addition, blizzard, compound, embrace, groove
V. accomplish, commotion, decorate, essential, marvelous
VI. bask, aisle, laborer, apparatus, amber
VII. rodeo, enumerate, immaculate, elementary, delusions
VIII. intelligent, wrest, vulnerable, debit, satchel

Test 26   CONTEXT CLUES

Example:

    A.   The boy had a black dog. He and his _____ dog played together.

        blond   black   white

    B.   The girl pulled her chin up and over the bar. She _____ herself.

        chimes   jumped   chinned

I

A.   Please give me another cookie. I need _____ glass of milk to go with the cookie.
    cookie   another   anything

B.   It looked like the rabbits were taking little jumps. I think you could say they _____.
    hopped   hoped   talked

C.   Do not feel sad. Let me dry your eyes. Please do not be _____ .
    unhappy   glad   carefree

D.   We saw a gateless fence but I want a fence with a _____ .
    fence   garter   gate

E.   In winter it does not rain. Sometime you may see _____ falling if you live high enough up in these mountains.
    snip   snow   rain

II.

A.   For our picnic let's take along some pop. It may get cold out. Let's bring _____ our sweaters too.

    along   away   picnic

B.   Apples, peaches, oranges, plums and bananas have seeds in them. They have a skin on the outside. They are _____ .

    frozen   fruit   animals

Test 26 (cont.)

C. John was fast in getting his work done. You could say he was _____ .

    quiet   rapidly   quick

D. It may be that no one can learn anything that he cannot _____ himself.

    teach   taken   bugle

E. Sometime when everyone is very quiet in the classroom you can hear the _____ of the clock.

    touch   search   ticking

III.

A. There is a smudge on your cheek. Wash your _____ before someone notices it.

    smooth   cheek   check

B. Can you explain why you were late? You must have had some _____ for being late.

    x-ray   rather   reason

C. Draw me a simple picture. Just a _____ picture will do.

    please   plain   pretty

D. Dry ice feels as though it will burn you but it will _____ you instead.

    freeze   tickle   scorch

E. Use this _____ to cut the bread with. It will work better than the old one.

    knives   knife   knee

IV.

A. Use a machine for the addition in these problems. _____ by hand is too slow.

    Add   Addition   Mechanize

B. The wind howled. It blew the snow drifts as high as a house. And still the snow came, blinding everyone in its path. It was the worst _____ in years.

    blizzard   blink   shower

C. When rail and road are joined you have a _____ word.

    complete   compound   bulky

D. Why some people shun one person and _____ another is not always easy to understand.

    embrace   repulse   avoid

Test 26 (cont.)

E. Some pieces of wood are called tongue and _____ because one part fits securely into the other.

    great   bit   groove

V.

A. You can accomplish great acts frequently by working harder than anyone else. You can _____ very little by mediocre effort.

    accompany   accomplish   merit

B. When the teacher leaves the room, erasers may be thrown, children talk, and someone may run around the room. This is the _____ the teacher may find when she returns.

    commotion   common   calm

C. Adding designs on your arithmetic paper may trim and even _____ it but the designs will not help to make the problems right.

    deteriorate   decorate   secret

D. The astronauts are not permitted to take nonessential things with them. They are permitted only _____ things.

    ascent   essence   essential

E. Some artists create _____ pictures.

    marvelous   malady   descenders

VI.

A. When you have done something well, it is right that you should bask in the glory of a job well done. You may even _____ in the glory of an achievement of a close relative.

    bask   bake   earn

B. Leave a row free of chairs in the middle of the room as an _____ .

    airspace   design   aisle

C. A workman who drives a truck is often referred to as a _____ .

    tramp   slicker   laborer

D. I have nothing with which to perform this experiment. Do you have the _____ that I could borrow?

    apparatus   apparent   space

E. The _____ stone has a yellowish hue.

    amber   ruby   diamond

Test 26 (cont.)

VII.

A. Rodeos generate a great deal of interest. This is why Wyoming has an annual
_____ .

      rodeo   aquatenniel   race

B. Write down in sequence the beauty spots — one, two, three, and four — that you have
seen. If you _____ them I won't be so apt to suggest a place that you've already
seen.

      limerick   beauty   enumerate

C. Her house was spotless. It was indeed _____ .

      immaculate   ubiquitous   tarnished

D. Sherlock Holmes in solving detective mysteries did not consider things as complicated
but rather as _____ .

      intricate   involved   elementary

E. He had _____ of grandeur when in fact he was poverty stricken.

      delusions   luminaries   falsities

VIII.

A. He was an intelligent boy in our class and in a comparable way she was an _____
girl.

      dull   quiet   intelligent

B. Somehow he had to eke out, cajole, or wring out a whole lifetime of knowledge from
that tiny little volume. How he could possibly _____ so much from so miniscule a
source was a miracle.

      wrest   rest   write

C. We are weak or _____ as teachers in the area about which we have the least
knowledge.

      vapid   vulnerable   valuable

D. This amount is entered on the wrong side of the ledger. It is a credit, not a _____ .

      defunct   debit   asset

E. The traveler opened his _____ .

      satchel   valiant   scepter

Test 27   NOUNS OUT

Description: Nouns Out is a cloze technique in which nouns are deleted. Insofar as possible, predictable nouns are the only ones omitted. Sentences progress from simple "actor-action" sentences to more involved structures.

This test is designed to assess the student's ability to use context clues as an aid to selecting the correct noun. (See pages 146-147.)

Appropriate for: students who score low on either Test 25 or Test 26.

Ages: 6 years 6 months to 13 years.

Testing Time: 10 minutes.

Directions for Use:
1. Administer the test individually with oral responses or to a whole class with written responses.
2. Be sure students understand the example before proceeding with the seven sets of multiple-choice sentence completions.
3. Stop testing with 4 incorrect out of 5 items.

Scoring the Test: See the following key for answers to the 35 test items. Expected scores are shown in the following chart:

	Grade Placement	Expected Scores
(Feb.-June)	1^2	3-5
	2	6-10
	3	11-15
	4	16-20
	5	21-25
	6	26-30
	7	31-35
	8	36-40

Remediation: Students who score 4 or more points below the expected scores for their grade need a program emphasizing nouns. Cloze exercises can be constructed by the teacher in which nouns are deleted to be filled in by the student.

Answer Key

1-5 Ducks, Dogs, Fish, Birds, Cats
6-10 Cows, Sheep, Hens, Fruits, Farmers
11-15 Umbrellas, Trees, Forests, Lumbermen, Lumber

16-20
Forks
Pots
Plates
Pitchers
Knives

21-25
lions
burros
Elephants
Anteaters
Antlers

26-30
hobby
box
cameramen
photography
picture

31-35
building
city
density
hunger
drowning

Test 27   NOUNS OUT

Name _____ Grade _____   Chronological Age _____

Date _____ Examiner _____   Score _____ out of 35
                                                                        yr.   mo.

Observations: _____
_____
_____

Example: _____ baa.

          _____ cluck.

Hens	Sheep
Cats	Beavers

Fill in the following blanks with a word that makes sense. Select this word from among those listed opposite the sentences.

1. _____ quack.
2. _____ bark.
3. _____ swim.
4. _____ fly.
5. _____ purr.

Dogs	Ducks
Cats	Snails
Birds	Fish

Fruits	Cows
Farmers	Sheep
Bees	Hens

6. _____ give milk.
7. _____ grow wool.
8. _____ lay eggs.
9. _____ grow on trees.
10. _____ work on the farm.

11. _____ keep off the rain.
12. _____ grow in forests.
13. _____ are made up of many trees.
14. _____ cut trees for lumber.
15. _____ is used to build houses.

Trees	Umbrellas
Forests	Lumber
Furniture	Lumbermen

Test 27 (cont.)

"Fill in the following blanks with words that make sense."

16. _____ are for eating meat.
17. _____ often hold coffee.
18. _____ usually hold our dinner.
19. _____ often hold milk.
20. _____ are for cutting meat.

Pots	Pitchers
Knives	Plates
Jams	Forks

21. Ferocious _____ and tigers belong to the cat family.
22. Little _____ and mules are related to the horse family.
23. _____ are huge land animals and they have big trunks.
24. _____ have long noses and eat ants.
25. _____ are found on animals belonging to the deer family.

Anteaters	Dove
lions	Elephants
burros	Antlers

26. Taking pictures on weekends is an expensive _____ .
27. Possibly the cheapest camera can be made from an old black _____ with a pinhole in it.
28. Professional _____ need expensive equipment.
29. Amateurs in the art of _____ usually have inexpensive cameras.
30. One _____ is said to be worth a thousand words.

cameramen	box
hobby	picture
photography	book

31. The Empire State Building used to be the tallest _____ in North America.
32. Los Angeles now is the biggest _____ in the United States.
33. People often dislike the crowded conditions of cities with high _____ .
34. In famines people die of _____.
35. In floods people die of _____.

starvation	building
drowning	density
city	hunger

Test 28   VERBS OUT

Description: Verbs Out is a cloze technique in which verbs are deleted. Insofar as possible only predictable verbs are omitted.

This test is designed to assess the student's ability to use context clues as an aid to selecting the correct verb. (See pages 150-151.)

Appropriate for: students who score low on Tests 25, 26, and/or 27.

Ages: 6 years 6 months through 13 years, or older students with reading disabilities.

Testing Time: 10 minutes.

Directions for Use:
1. Administer the test individually with oral responses or to a whole class with written responses.
2. Be sure students understand the example before proceeding with the test.
3. Stop testing with 4 errors out of 5 consecutive items.

Scoring the Test: See the following key for answers to the eight sets of sentence completions. Expected performance is as follows:

	Grade Placement	Expected Score
(Feb.-June)	1^2	3-5
	2	5-10
	3	11-15
	4	16-20
	5	21-25
	6	26-30
	7	31-35
	8	36-40

Remediation: Students who score 4 or more points below the expected scores for their grade need a program emphasizing verbs. The teacher can construct cloze exercises in which verbs are deleted to be filled in by the student.

1. quack
   bark
   swim
   fly
   purr

2. give
   catch
   lay
   grow
   work

3. give
   grow
   are
   cut
   is

4. hold
   pour
   Pass
   are
   like

5. skid
   slide
   cut
   tied
   closes

6. take
   paint
   mold
   swim
   fly

7. climb
   run
   design
   build
   paint

8. decorate
   sew
   perform
   dig
   study

Test 28 VERBS OUT

Name _____ Grade _____ Chronological Age _____
                                                              yr.   mo.
Date _____ Examiner _____ Total Correct _____
        _____ Expected Score _____
        _____ Above _____ Below _____
        _____ Average _____

Example: Hens _____ | sing   cluck |
             Sheep _____ | baa   write |

Fill in the following blanks with a word that makes sense. Select this word from among those listed opposite the sentences.

1.

Ducks _____ | fly   bark |
Dogs _____ | quack   skate |
Fish _____ | swim   purr |
Birds _____
Cats _____

| grow   grant |
| work   lay |
| give   catch |

2.
Cows _____ milk.
Cats _____ mice.
Hens _____ eggs.
Leaves _____ on trees.
Farmers _____ on their farms.

3.
Trees _____ us shade.
Trees _____ in forests.
Forests _____ made up of trees.
Lumbermen _____ trees for lumber.
Lumber _____ used to build houses.

| give   is |
| are   dance |
| cut   grow |

Test 28 (cont.)

Fill in the following blanks with words that make sense.

4.
Cups often _____ coffee.
Please _____ milk in my glass.
_____ me the potatoes, please.
Knives _____ for cutting meat.
I _____ ice cream best.

Pass	hold
Put	pour
are	like

skid	lied
cut	tied
closes	slide

5.
Cars _____ on wet ice.
Sleds _____ on hard snow.
Sharp skates _____ the ice.
Tennis laces need to be _____ .
A zippered jacket _____ rapidly.

6.
You can _____ pictures with your camera.
You can _____ with water colors.
You can _____ with clay.
You can _____ in this pool.
You can _____ this kite.

paint	mold
take	sleep
swim	fly

7.
Mountaineers can _____ mountains.
Railroad engineers usually _____ trains.
Architects _____ buildings.
Contractors _____ buildings.
Painters _____ buildings.

ruin	paint
build	design
run	climb

8.
Interior decorators _____ buildings.
Seamstresses _____ clothes.
Clowns _____ for a living.
Coal miners _____ for a living.
Students _____ to earn good grades.

perform	study
sew	dig
decorate	sing

Test 29   ADJECTIVES OUT

Description: Adjectives Out is a cloze technique in which adjectives are deleted. As a guide in this test, each group of adjectives is preceded by such signal words as color, size, and taste. (See pages 154-155.)

Appropriate for: students who score low on Tests 25, 26, 27, and/or 28.

Ages: 6 years 6 months through 14 years.

Testing Time: 10 minutes.

Directions for Use:
1. Administer the test to small groups or to the whole class.
2. Be sure students can correctly mark the example before proceeding with the test.
3. Stop testing at 4 errors out of 5 consecutive items.

Scoring the Test: See the following key for answers to the nine sets of exercises. Guidelines to expected performance are as follows:

	Grade Placement	Expected Scores
(Feb.-June)	1^2	1-3
	2	3-5
	3	6-10
	4	11-15
	5	16-20
	6	21-25
	7	26-30
	8	31-35
	9	36-40

Remediation: Students who score 4 or more points below the expected scores for their grade placement need a program patterned after the sentences in this test.

Answer Key

NOTE: Accept any *logical* adjectives. The most commonly given answers are listed here.

1/2. red
   green, blue
   red
   blue
   white
   yellow

3. tall, big, lanky
   little, small
   big, huge, gigantic
   skinny, thin
   small, tiny, little

4. sour, bitter, unripe, moldy
   sweet, cinnamon
   bitter
   salty
   fishy, bitter, bad, rancid, strong

5. soft, fluffy
   rough, harsh
   stiff
   sharp
   soft, smooth, silky

6. queenly
   majestic
   humorous
   cuddly
   frisky

7. water-based
   gigantic
   long-nosed
   curly
   poisonous

8. democratic
   communistic
   fascist
   independent
   modified

9. law-making
   executive
   law-enforcement
   juvenile
   highest

Test 29 Adjectives Out

Please fill in the appropriate word in the blanks —
Example: This _____ suit is Santa's.

1/2. Color

The _____ grass is pretty.
The _____ rubies are beautiful.
The _____ sky is clear.
The _____ snow is clean.
This _____ banana is ripe.

yellow
white
green, blue
red
blue

skinny, thin
tall, big, lanky
little, small
small, little, tiny
big, huge, gigantic

3. Size

The _____ boy is almost 7 feet.
The _____ girl is just 3 feet.
The _____ lady weighs over 200 pounds.
The _____ man is tall but weighs only 90 pounds.
The _____ baby weighs 6 pounds.

4. Taste

This _____ lemon is not good.
This _____ roll is good.
This _____ coffee is too strong.
This _____ popcorn makes me thirsty.
This tuna tastes too _____ .

salty
bitter
fishy, bitter, bad, rancid, strong
sour, bitter, unripe, moldy
sweet, cinnamon

rough, harsh
sharp
soft, fluffy
soft, smooth, silky
stiff

5. Texture

Cotton is _____ .
Sandpaper is _____ .
Starch makes clothes _____ .
Rose thorns are _____ .
Satin feels _____ .

Test 29 (cont.)

6. Attributes

The queen is _____ .
The king is _____ .
The court jester is _____ .
The baby is _____ .
The colt is _____ .

```
majestic
queenly
cuddly
humorous
frisky
```

```
curly
poisonous
gigantic
long-nosed
water-based
```

7. Attributes

The alligator is _____ .
The hippopotamus is _____ .
The warthog is _____ .
The pig has a _____ tail.
Some snakes are _____ .

8. Types of Rule

The United States is a _____ country.
Russia is a _____ country.
Spain is a _____ state.
Most of Africa has _____ countries.
Monarchies exist in _____ form.

```
modified
democratic
fascist
communistic
independent
```

```
executive
law-making
highest
juvenile
law-enforcement
```

9. Functions

Parliament is the _____ body in Britain.
The President and his cabinet form the _____ branch of government in the United States.
The courts are a part of the _____ agency in the U.S.
The court for children is known as a _____ court.
The United States Supreme Court is the _____ court in the country.

Test 30 JUMBLED SENTENCES

Description: This test consists of 11 scrambled sentences followed by 4 multiple choices: one totally incorrect response (foil), one correctly unscrambled version, one negative form of scrambled sentence, and one interrogative form of the unscrambled sentence. (See pages 158-160.) The test is a measure of the student's recognition of the importance of syntax and of the ability to recognize negative and interrogative sentences generated from a declarative sentence.

Appropriate for: students who score low in comprehension but who are able to pass Tests 26 through 28.

Ages: 6 years 6 months through 16 years.

Testing Time: 10 minutes.

Directions for Use:
1. Administer the test as a group test.
2. Be sure students understand the example before proceeding with the test items.
3. Proceed as follows:
   a. "Find the unscrambled sentence and mark it _/_ ."
   b. "Find the negative statement to match and mark it _No._"
   c. "Find the interrogative sentence (question) to match and mark it_ ? _ "
   d. "Leave the totally incorrect sentence blank."

Scoring the Test: See the following key for answers to the test items. Score 2 points for each correctly marked sentence.

	Grade	*Expected Scores*
(Feb.-June)	1^2	2-4
	2	6-8
	3	10-14
	4	16-20
	5	22-26
	6	28-32
	7	34-38
	8	40-44
	9	46-50
	10	52-56
	11	58-62

Remediation: Students who score 4 or more points below the expected scores for their grade placement need some additional practice with exercises similar to those found in this test. There is a helpful class exercise in which students make up three sentences on a half sheet of paper, and on the lower half write the same sentences out of order. Papers are then folded in half with the scrambled sentences placed on top. Students then exchange papers and each student tries to unscramble his three sentences and re-write them in the correct order within three minutes. At the end of this time, students can unfold their papers and check their answers with the sentences found on the top halves of their papers.

Answer Key

A.	/	4
	?	3
	No	1

B.	/	2
	?	4
	No	1

C.	/	2
	?	3
	No	4

D.	/	1
	?	2
	No	4

E.	/	3
	?	4
	No	2

F.	/	3
	?	4
	No	1

G.	/	3
	?	4
	No	1

H.	/	3
	?	1
	No	4

I.	/	4
	?	3
	No	1

J.	/	2
	?	1
	No	4

K.	/	1
	?	2
	No	3

NOTE: Unscrambling sentences emphasizes the importance of syntax or word order. Generating negative and interrogative forms emphasizes the relationship between sentences.

Test 30   JUMBLED SENTENCES

(Syntax and Recognition of Generated Interrogative and Negative Sentences)

Name _____ Grade _____   Chronological Age _____

_____ yr.   mo.

Date _____ Examiner _____

Observations: _____   Scores:

_____   Unscrambled _____

_____   Interrogative _____

_____   Negative _____

_____   Average _____

_____   Above _____ Below _____

PLACE THE CORRECT CODE MARK GIVEN BELOW IN BLANKS PROVIDED
FOR THIS PURPOSE. Study the Example to be found to right of CODE.

CODE   EXAMPLE: Ex.   can   go   I

Unscrambled   /   /   3   _____ 1. Can I go
Interrogative ?   ?   1   _____ 2. Will I go
Negative   No   No   4   _____ 3. I can go
                                        _____ 4. I can't go

A. jump I can

    /_____◆   _____ 1. I can't jump
    ?_____   _____ 2. You can't jump
    No_____   _____ 3. Can I jump
                     _____ 4. I can jump

B. drinking You are

    /_____   _____ 1. You aren't drinking
    ?_____   _____ 2. You are drinking
    No_____   _____ 3. You weren't drinking
                     _____ 4. Are you drinking

C. played We have here

    /_____   _____ 1. We are playing here
    ?_____   _____ 2. We have played here
    No_____   _____ 3. Have we played here
                     _____ 4. We haven't played here

D. my They are graphs

    /_____   _____ 1. They are my graphs
    ?_____   _____ 2. Are they my graphs
    No_____   _____ 3. Are they your graphs
                     _____ 4. They aren't my graphs

E. excellent biology has He in grades

    /_____   _____ 1. He hasn't any grade in biology excellent
    ?_____   _____ 2. He doesn't have excellent grades in biology
    No_____   _____ 3. He has excellent grades in biology
                     _____ 4. Does he have excellent grades in biology

Test 30 (cont.)

F. brown   eyes   hair   curly   and   He   has   has   he

/ _____   _____ 1.   He hasn't got brown eyes and curly hair

? _____   _____ 2.   He has curly eye lashes and brown hair

No _____   _____ 3.   He has brown eyes and he has curly hair

                  _____ 4.   Has he got brown eyes and curly hair

G. the   victim   When   the   ambulance   arrived   was   in   shock

/ _____   _____ 1.   When the ambulance arrived the victim was not in
                               in shock

? _____   _____ 2.   When the victim arrived the ambulance was in shock

No _____   _____ 3.   When the ambulance arrived, the victim was in shock

                  _____ 4.   Was the victim in shock when the ambulance arrived

H. the   enemy   reasoned   At   twilight   the   Minutemen   we   can   stalk   on
   their   own   land

/ _____   _____ 1.   At twilight the enemy reasoned can we stalk the
                               Minutemen on their own land

? _____   _____ 2.   At twilight the enemy reasoned we can stalk the
                               enemy on their own land

No _____   _____ 3.   At twilight the enemy reasoned we can stalk the
                               Minutemen on their own land

                  _____ 4.   At twilight the enemy reasoned we can't stalk the
                               enemy on their own land.

I. the   temperature   When   the   sun   sets   red   is   hot   on   the   following   day

/ _____   _____ 1.   When the sun sets red the temperature on the follow-
                               ing day is not hot

? _____   _____ 2.   When the sun sets red the temperature prediction is
                               uncertain

No _____   _____ 3.   When the sun sets red is the temperature hot on the
                               following day

                  _____ 4.   When the sun sets red the temperature on the
                               following day is hot

J. the   boat   was   becalmed   Just   before   the   storm   was   motionless   and
   without   a   motor

/ _____   _____ 1.   Just before the storm was the boat becalmed and
                               without a motor was it motionless

? _____   _____ 2.   Just before the storm the boat was becalmed and
                               without a motor was motionless

No _____   _____ 3.   Just before the boat the storm was becalmed and
                               even without a motor it was not motionless

                  _____ 4.   Just before the storm the boat was not becalmed and
                               without a motor it was not motionless

Test 30 (cont.)

K. saw Faithful club members the sailboats off at San Diego to Ensenada to watch finish the race the boats and then drove down

<u>/</u>

<u>?</u>

<u>No</u>

———— 1. Faithful club members saw the sailboats off at San Diego and then drove down to Ensenado to watch the boats finish the race

———— 2. Did faithful club members see the sailabots off at San Deigo and then drive down to Ensenado to watch the boats finish the race

———— 3. Faithful club members did not see the sailboats off at San Diego and didn't drive down to Ensenado to watch the boats finish the race

———— 4. Faithful club members saw the sailboats off at Ensenada and then drove down to San Diego to watch the boats finish the race

Test 31 CULTURAL SAMPLING

Description: This test consists of 40 references to our cultural heritage — 10 made up of "old sayings,"10 mythical references, 10 from fables, and 10 from our history. (See pages 162-164.) Students are required to choose a common meaning to match the cultural sampling.

Appropriate for: students of all types. It is particularly helpful to assess students who are not native or who are native but who have spent a number of years in foreign countries (e.g., servicemen's families).

Ages: 11 through 16, and older students with reading disabilities.

Testing Time: 8 minutes.

Directions for Use:

Scoring: See the following key for answers to the 40 test items.

As in most tests the total score is of less value than discovering the pattern of what is known and what needs to be taught. For example, a student who misses only the mythical references can be directed to read an appropriate collection of myths.

Answer Key

Old Sayings		Fable References	
	3		2
	9		1
	1		5
	4		3
	6		4
	2		9
	7		6
	5		8
	10		7
	8		10

Mythical References		Historical References	
	2		2
	1		1
	7		3
	5		10
	3		4
	4		9
	6		5
	10		8
	9		6
	8		7

Test 31   Cultural Sampling

Name _____ Grade _____   Chronological Age _____

Date _____ Examiner _____

Observations: _____

_____

_____

Score: Old Sayings __ out of 10
Mythical _____ out of 10
Historical _____ out of 10
TOTAL _____ out of 30

yr.   mo.

Example:

_____ To err is human,
To forgive divine.

1. Everyone makes mistakes but the person who forgives seems immortal or divine.
2. Everyone makes mistakes but divine immortal persons forgive and are therefore to be admired.

Old Sayings:

_____ Every cloud has a silver lining.

_____ The early bird gets the worm.

_____ A rolling stone gathers no moss.

_____ A bird in the hand is worth two in the bush.

_____ It never rains but it pours.

_____ No news is good news.

_____ Hope springs eternal.

_____ Silence is golden.

_____ Wait until your ship comes in.

_____ Opportunity knocks but once.

1. One who is always on the move does not accumulate anything.
2. No news at all allows one to continue hoping for good news.
3. Every misfortune has something good about it.
4. Do not give up what is already owned for what looks like more but is uncertain.
5. There are times when absolute silence is prized.
6. If one unlucky thing happens, watch out. There may be more.
7. Hope does not die with an advance of age.
8. Take advantage of opportunity or you may never have another chance.
9. The person who is first to respond is likely to get the job.
10. Refers to making a lot of money.

Test 31 (cont.)

Mythical References:

_____ Pandora's Box
_____ Achilles' Heel
_____ Winged Victory
_____ Cupid's Arrow
_____ Atlas
_____ Adonis
_____ Venus
_____ Atlanta
_____ Pygmalion
_____ Narcissus

1. One's weakest spot
2. Despair, hate, jealousy, and hope
3. Inordinate strength
4. A handsome man
5. Smitten by love
6. Womanly beauty
7. With amazing speed
8. One filled with self-love
9. In love with an ideal statue which came to life
10. A superior woman tricked to defeat by 3 golden apples

References from Fables:

_____ Wolf! Wolf!

_____ Sour grapes!

_____ Hare and the Tortoise

_____ Grasshopper and the Ant
_____ Androcles and the Lion
_____ The Bundle of Sticks
_____ The Miller, His Son and the Donkey
_____ The Country Mouse and the City Mouse
_____ The Goose that laid the Golden Eggs
_____ The Miser

1. People tend to "run down" that which they cannot have.
2. Those who ask for help when they do not need it are not likely to be given help when they DO need it.
3. One needs to plan and work for the future.
4. A noble deed is not forgotten.
5. Slow and sure is better than fast and over-confident.
6. Don't try to please everyone or you'll please NO one.
7. Don't be too greedy or you may end up with nothing.
8. Crusts eaten in peace are better than cakes eaten in fear.
9. There is strength in sticking together.
10. Money has no true value unless it is used.

Test 31 (cont.)

Historical References:

_____ Abraham Lincoln

_____ Benedict Arnold

_____ John Alden

_____ J.F. Kennedy

_____ Betsy Ross

_____ Woodrow Wilson

_____ Harriet Tubman

_____ Teddy Roosevelt

_____ Winston Churchill

_____ Paul Revere

1. A traitor
2. One who abolished slavery
3. One who asked Pricilla for her hand in the name of Captain Smith
4. A brave woman who made flags
5. A freedom fighter
6. The Prime Minister of England during the Second World War
7. He rode to warn the Colonists of the arrival of the British soldiers
8. Captain of the Rough Riders
9. He dreamed up the League of Nations
10. A 20th century President of the United States who was assassinated while in office

Section VI Summary

Tests in this section are concerned with syntax and semantics. Test 25 requires the student to match sentences that have been reworded. This test of comprehension is a measure of a skill needed as a frequently used study tool. Test 26 gives the diagnostician a chance to isolate any one of five types of context clues:

1. word already used
2. word defined
3. synonym given
4. antonym given
5. from experience, vicarious or real

Tests 27, 28, and 29 give the diagnostician a chance to look at whichever part of speech (noun, verb, or adjective) causes the student the most difficulty.

Test 30, jumbled sentences, tests the student's knowledge of correct word order or syntax, and his ability to recognize generated interrogative and negative sentences.

Test 31 is a cultural sampling of the student's knowledge of "old sayings," fables, myths, and history.

All of the tests in this section involve sentences and stress comprehension. They are included because it seems important that students be able to comprehend at the sentence level in order to understand material at the paragraph level and beyond.

References

Forgan, Harry W. *The Reading Corner: Ideas, Games and Activities for Individualizing Reading,* Santa Monica, Ca.: Goodyear Publishing Co., 1977.

Gerhard, Christian. *Making Sense: Reading Comprehension Improved Through Categorizing.* Newark, Del.: International Reading Association, 1975.

Griese, Arnold A., *Do You Read Me?* Practical Approaches to Teaching Reading Comprehension, Santa Monica, Ca.: Goodyear Publishing Co., 1977.

Guthrie, J.T., "Reading Comprehension and Syntactic Responses in Good and Poor Readers," *Journal of Educational Psychology,* Vol. 65, No. 3 (1973), 294-300.

Guthrie, J.T. *et al.,* "The Maze Technique to Assess, Monitor Reading Comprehension," *The Reading Teacher,* Nov. 1974.

Heilman, Arthur W. and Holmes, Elizabeth A. *Smuggling Language into the Teaching of Reading.* Columbus, Ohio: Merrill, 1972.

Robinson, Richard D. *An Introduction to the Cloze Procedure* (Annotated Bibliography). Newark, Del.: International Reading Association, 1972.

Schulwitz, Bonnie S. *Teachers, Tangibles, Techniques: Comprehension of Content in Reading.* Newark, Del.: International Reading Association, 1975.

Spache, Evelyn B. *Reading Activities for Child Involvement.* Rockleigh, N.J.: Allyn and Bacon, Inc., 1976.

Wilson, Robert M., "Comprehension Diagnosis Via Task Analysis," *Reading World,* Vol. 14, No. 3 (March, 1975), 178-179.

SECTION VII

measuring paragraph skills

(Contains Tests 32 through 37)

The focus in this section is on the next language structural unit, the paragraph. In our measurement of paragraph skills, we are still concerned with meaning at all levels — word, phrase, and sentence — though in a broader framework. It is possible for paragraph comprehension to be slowed down or blocked by an unknown word, an incorrect phrase, and/or a sentence that needs interpretation. Like seasoning in cooking, words in paragraphs permeate, temper, and control the flavor and intent just as they influence one another. For example, take the simple word "bar." This could refer to the usage made by Tennyson in his poem in which "crossing the bar" refers to death. True, this is an unusual use of the word, but the strength of CONTEXT as a controller of meaning is obvious.

Tests in this section are designed to measure a student's sensitivity to context clues, topic sentences, and his or her ability to anticipate words. Table VIII provides a brief overview.

Table VIII
Test Guide 32-37

Test	Title	Ages	Minutes	Appropriate for students who:
32	San Diego Quick Oral Paragraphs Form I	6-15	8	are 6 and/or who pass the SDQA at the first reader level or above
33	San Diego Quick Oral Paragraphs Form II	6-15	8	are 6 and/or who pass the SDQA at the first reader level or above
34	Topic Sentences	8-16	10	have difficulty in keeping their attention on what they read
35	Modified Cloze	5-13	10	have a better vocabulary of words in isolation than in context
36	Maze/Comprehension	7-15	10	need to have comprehension skills measured and monitored
37	Quality of Comprehension	6-9	5	need to have an assessment of silent reading skills and listening skills

Test 32 SAN DIEGO QUICK ORAL PARAGRAPHS
Form I

Description: Each San Diego Quick Oral Paragraph Test contains the same 10 words found in the San Diego Quick Assessment graded word lists. (See pages 170-191.) Most of the additional words are of an easier readability level. The few words that might cause difficulty are adequately introduced as they are pictured and may be easily referred to.

Appropriate for: students whose level of oral reading skills is unknown. This test is useful when it is desirable to compare a student's skill in using words in isolation with the skill in reading identical words in context.

Ages: 6 through 15, or older students with reading disabilities.

Testing Time: 8 minutes.

Directions for Use:

To prepare for the test, duplicate copies of the oral paragraph cards in Appendix IV, pages 257-261. Place the cards in sequence either in a photograph album or two notebook rings for ease of use in testing.

Whenever possible, administer the San Diego Quick Assessment of Graded Words (SDQA, page 71) to discover the student's ability to pronounce words in isolation. Administer the oral paragraphs beginning at one grade level below the child's score on the graded word list.

Example:

> *Step 1* Administer the SDQA, Form I, which is a graded word list.
> Reader Level 2: Child substitutes *said* for *send*
>   *quickly* for *quietly*
> This places him at grade 2 as his instructional level.
> *Step 2* Have the child read paragraphs aloud at Preprimer Level 1, which is one grade below his SDQA reader level.
> *Step 3* Watch for: hesitations, repetitions, word substitution, lack of intonation, inattention to punctuation, unreasonable phrasing, lack of enthusiasm, voice strain, poor articulation, short eye-voice span, reading rate unrelated to normal speaking rate, and other anomalies.

Directions for presenting each level on both forms of the San Diego Quick Oral Paragraphs are provided on the student's record forms, pages 171-180 and 182-191. Test data should then be recorded and evaluated according to procedures on the Cover Sheets, pages 170 and 181.

Scoring the Test: It is essential in scoring this test that word substitutions be recorded *above* the stimulus word. In this manner the examiner gathers information as to the position and quality of errors — initial, medial, or final — and notes whether the errors are made at the whole word, syllable, consonant cluster, consonant or vowel level. Thus, in measuring word accuracy the student's substitutions are essential to an analysis of errors.

In all, there are three measures of word accuracy that are of interest:

1. words identical to the 10 on the SDQA.
2. any other words missed, including the missing of one of the 10 words repeated in the paragraph.
3. the total number missed in order to assess whether the number was within the passing limits for word accuracy.

NOTE: The TOTAL number of words the student can miss and still pass the paragraph in word accuracy is listed at the end of each paragraph. The ceiling level is the highest level passed in word accuracy.

Comprehension: The most common measure of comprehension is to recall in general what happened and to whom it happened. This is a daily task in reading the newspaper, magazines, and fiction. Even well-written social studies material requires the student to read for the main events and the persons involved. Because most of the student's reading tasks are to recall such events and characters, each paragraph is followed by a variation of these two questions:

What happened?
To whom did it happen?

Students who cannot recall the main event, who get it confused, or who remember the main event but cannot recall to whom it happened, fail to pass in comprehension.

Listening Comprehension Level: Try reading aloud to the student at the level in which failure in word accuracy and/or comprehension occurs. If the student is able to tell what happened and to whom, continue with the next higher paragraph until the student is NO LONGER able to recall either the main event and/or the characters.

Cover Sheet

Test 32   SAN DIEGO QUICK ORAL PARAGRAPHS
Form I

Name _____ Grade _____   Chronological Age _____
                                                              yr.   mo.
Date _____ Examiner _____   SDQA Reader Level _____
Observations: _____   Minus 1 Grade Level _____
_____   Entry Oral ¶ Level _____
_____   Ceiling Level _____
_____   Listening Level _____

Materials:a. S.D. Oral Paragraph cards cut and collated so that the student sees only 1 card
            at a time. See Appendix IV.
         b. Copies of Student's Record Forms.
         c. Copy of student's performance on the SDQA.

PROCEDURE: 1. Record data on this Cover Sheet.
           2. Read the prereading information on student record forms.
           3. Record under word accuracy all of the words missed: mispronounced, omitted
              or substituted. Be sure to write in the substitutions as they sound to you by
              using diacritical marks or phonetic spelling.

WORDS MISSED at TOP level of the SDQA	WORDS MISSED at the SAME level of Oral ¶	WORDS MISSED ON ORAL ¶ AT HIGHER LEVEL	WORDS MISSED ON ORAL ¶ AT LOWER LEVEL
_____	_____	_____	_____
_____	_____	_____	_____
_____	_____	_____	_____
_____	_____	_____	_____
_____	_____	_____	_____

✓ Check Appropriate Description:

_____scored _____ grade level(s) higher on the SD Oral Paragraphs than on the SDQA, and
      therefore USES CONTEXT CLUES AS AN EFFECTIVE READING STRATEGY.
_____scored _____ grade level(s) LOWER on the SD Oral Paragraphs than on the SDQA which
      suggests an OVEREMPHASIS ON PHONICS.
_____scored at the same grade level on the SD Oral Paragraphs as on the SDQA which suggests
      that the STUDENT HAS REACHED HIS INTELLECTUAL CAPACITY OR THAT
      NOT ENOUGH EMPHASIS HAS BEEN PLACED ON MEANING. (Children, typically,
      score higher on paragraphs because context clues aid them.)
RECOMMENDATIONS: _____
_____
_____
_____
_____

Test 32   SAN DIEGO ORAL PARAGRAPHS   FORM I

Reader Level: Preprimer

Note: Words underlined in the paragraphs are identical to those found on the San Diego
Quick Assessment Form I.

PREREADING: Look at this word — *ball*. Find it in the paragraph. Discuss baseball and how fast
one runs to make a *home* run.

Examiner: "READ THIS PARAGRAPH ALOUD. THINK ABOUT WHAT YOU ARE
READING. THEN TELL ME IN YOUR OWN WORDS WHAT HAPPENED AND TO
WHOM IT HAPPENED."

SEE ME PLAY BALL.

I CAN RUN.

LOOK AT ME GO.

I CAN RUN AND PLAY HERE.

LOOK AT ME RUN HOME.

22

COMPREHENSION: Record the student's retelling _____

_____

_____

_____

_____

WORD ACCURACY:

SUBSTITUTIONS   NUMBERS

Similar in sound
(ex. — a, the /ə/,/Ŏə/) .... _____ |____ Underlined words missed
Similar in meaning | _____ .... Other words missed
(ex. — big, large) .... _____ | _____ .... Total words missed
                                             | _____ ...... Perfect to 2 missed = Passed
                                             |____ _____ .... 3 or more missed = Failed

Test 32   SAN DIEGO ORAL PARAGRAPHS FORM 1

Reader Level: Primer

Note: Words underlined in the paragraphs are identical to those found on the San Diego Quick Assessment Form I.

PREREADING: Look carefully at the words *sail* and *boat*. Sailing a boat is usually *fun* and not work.

Examiner: "READ THIS PARAGRAPH ALOUD. THINK ABOUT WHAT YOU ARE READING: THEN TELL ME IN YOUR OWN WORDS WHAT HAPPENED AND TO WHOM IT HAPPENED."

"COME AND JUMP IN WITH ME.

THIS BOAT IS FUN.

YOU CAN HELP ME SAIL.

IT IS NOT WORK TO SAIL.

WE ARE IN A SAILBOAT."

26

COMPREHENSION: Record the student's retelling _____

_____

_____

_____

_____

WORD ACCURACY:

SUBSTITUTIONS   NUMBERS

Similar in sound

(ex. — a, the/ə/,/Óə/) .... _____|—— Underlined words missed

Similar in meaning |—— .... Other words missed

(ex. — big, large) .... _____|—— .... Total words missed

                                                 |—— .... Perfect to 3 missed = Passed

                                                 |—— .... 4 or more missed = Failed

Test 32   SAN DIEGO ORAL PARAGRAPHS FORM I

Reader Level: First

Note: words underlined in the paragraphs are identical to those found on the San Diego Quick Assessment Form I.

PREREADING: Look carefully at *walk* and *fish*. Discuss how much fun it is to go fishing and catch fish.

Examiner: "READ THIS PARAGRAPH ALOUD. THINK ABOUT WHAT YOU ARE READING. THEN TELL ME IN YOUR OWN WORDS WHAT HAPPENED AND TO WHOM IT HAPPENED."

> TODAY IS SPRING. WHEN SPRING IS HERE, I LIKE TO FISH.
>
> I LIVE BY A ROAD. I WALK ON THIS ROAD WHEN I WANT TO
>
> FISH. HOW THE DAY FLIES BY. I ALWAYS TRY FOR A BIGGER
>
> AND BIGGER FISH.
>
> IF I GET A BIG ONE, MOM WILL THANK ME. WE WILL EAT IT
>
> THIS NIGHT.   56

COMPREHENSION: Record the student's retelling_____

_____

_____

_____

_____

WORD ACCURACY:

SUBSTITUTIONS   NUMBERS

Similar in sound

  (ex. — a, the/ə/,/Ŏə) .... _____ |___ Underline words missed

Similar in meaning |___ .... Other words missed

  (ex. — big, large) .... _____ |___ .... Total words missed

                                   |___ ... Perfect to 6 missed = Passed

                                   |___ ..... 7 or more missed = Failed

Test 32   SAN DIEGO ORAL PARAGRAPHS   FORM I

Reader Level: Second

Note: Words underlined in the paragraphs are identical to those found on the San Diego
      Quick Assessment Form I.

PREREADING: Look at this word — *block*. Discuss the fact that parents don't usually like
children to make banging noises early in the morning.

Examiner: "READ THIS PARAGRAPH ALOUD. THINK ABOUT WHAT YOU ARE
      READING. THEN TELL ME IN YOUR OWN WORDS WHAT HAPPENED AND TO
      WHOM IT HAPPENED."

I MADE THIS BLOCK <u>TOWN</u> TO <u>PLEASE</u> <u>MYSELF</u>. I GOT UP

<u>EARLY</u> AND WORKED QUIETLY. I MADE A <u>WIDE</u> ROAD. THEN, I

<u>CAREFULLY</u> PUT BLOCK ON BLOCK. I <u>BELIEVE</u> IT WILL NOT

FALL DOWN.

    <u>OUR</u> HOUSE IS QUIET TODAY. I AM WORKING <u>QUIETLY</u> AND

CAREFULLY. MOTHER WILL NOT <u>SEND</u> ME OUT TO PLAY.

53

COMPREHENSION: Record the student's retelling _____

_____

_____

_____

_____

<u>WORD</u> <u>ACCURACY</u>:

SUBSTITUTIONS   NUMBERS

Similar in sound
  (ex. — a, the /ə/,/Óə/) .... ____ |____ Underlined words missed
Similar in meaning
  (ex. — big, large) .... ____ |............... Other words missed
                                  |............... Total words missed
                                    |____ ...... Perfect to 5 missed = Passed
                                    |____ .... 6 or more missed = Failed

Test 32 *SAN DIEGO ORAL PARAGRAPHS* FORM I

Reader Level: Third

Note: Words underlined in the paragraphs are identical to those found on the San Diego
     Quick Assessment Form I.

PREREADING: Have you ever been lost in a strange city? If so, how did it feel? If not, how do you
     think it would feel?

Examiner: "READ THIS PARAGRAPH ALOUD. THINK ABOUT WHAT YOU ARE
     READING. THEN TELL ME IN YOUR OWN WORDS WHAT HAPPENED AND TO
     WHOM IT HAPPENED."

THE BOY LOOKED FRIGHTENED. HE WAS IN THE MIDDLE OF

THE WALK. HE LOOKED LONELY IN THE CITY AS THE CARS

ZOOMED BY.

IN A MOMENT, SEVERAL MEN WALKED PAST.

A TALL MAN DREW UP IN A CAR. HE GOT OUT AND WALKED

STRAIGHT TO THE BOY.

"WHY AREN'T YOU IN SCHOOL?" THE MAN EXCLAIMED.

SINCE THE BOY DID NOT KNOW WHAT TO SAY, HE BEGAN TO

CRY.   68

COMPREHENSION: Record the student's retelling _____

_____

_____

WORD ACCURACY:

SUBSTITUTIONS   NUMBERS

Similar in sound
  (ex. — a, the /ə/,/ŏə/) .... _____|_____ Underlined words missed
Similar in meaning |......... .... Other words missed
  (ex. — big, large) .... _____|_____ .... Total words missed
                                            |...... Perfect to 7 missed = Passed
                                            |......... 8 or more missed = Failed

Test 32 SAN DIEGO ORAL PARAGRAPHS FORM I

Reader Level: Fourth

Note: Words underlined in the paragraphs are identical to those found on the San Diego Quick Assessment Form I.

PREREADING: Look at this word — *rock*. Discuss what would happen if you skated into a rock.

Examiner: "READ THIS PARAGRAPH ALOUD. THINK ABOUT WHAT YOU ARE READING. THEN TELL ME IN YOUR OWN WORDS WHAT HAPPENED AND TO WHOM IT HAPPENED."

A BOY <u>DECIDED</u> TO <u>IMPROVE</u> THE CAR HE WAS MAKING. IT WAS NOT A <u>SILENT</u> CAR, BUT IT <u>SERVED</u> HIM WELL. IT <u>CERTAINLY</u> WASN'T A RACING CAR, BUT GOING DOWNHILL IT WAS FAST.

THE BOY <u>ENTERED</u> A DOWNHILL RACE. HE <u>REALIZED</u> HIS CAR WAS NOT A RACE CAR. STILL HE WANTED TO TRY.

ON THE DAY OF THE RACE, HIS CAR <u>AMAZED</u> HIM, AND HE WAS PLEASED. IT WENT SO FAST DOWNHILL, HE MIGHT HAVE WON, BUT THE RACE WAS <u>INTERRUPTED</u>. HIS CAR HIT A ROCK AND WAS <u>WRECKED</u>.

22

COMPREHENSION: Record the student's retelling _____

_____

_____

<u>WORD ACCURACY:</u>

SUBSTITUTIONS   NUMBERS

Similar in sound
(ex. — a, the /ə/, /ŏə/) .... _____ | _____ Underlined words missed
Similar in meaning | _____ .... Other words missed
(ex. — big, large) .... _____ | _____ .... Total words missed
                                                | _____ ...... Perfect to 9 missed = Passed
                                                | _____ .... 10 or more missed = Failed

Test 32 *SAN DIEGO ORAL PARAGRAPHS* FORM I

Reader Level: Fifth

Note: Words underlined in the paragraphs are identical to those found on the San Diego Quick Assessment Form I.

PREREADING: Look at the words *knot* and *listened.* Discuss Halloween night and why fat people often like treats.

Examiner: "READ THIS PARAGRAPH ALOUD. THINK ABOUT WHAT YOU ARE READING. THEN TELL ME IN YOUR OWN WORDS WHAT HAPPENED AND TO WHOM IT HAPPENED."

THE THREE BOYS WERE TIED UP AS A HALLOWEEN TRICK BY A BADLY BEHAVED GANG.

"SOMETHING WILL DEVELOP," ONE OF THE BOYS SAID, AS THEY DISCUSSED HOW TO ESCAPE.

"WE HAVE A SCANTY CHANCE," ANOTHER BOY SAID SADLY.

"I'VE ESCAPED FROM OTHER TIE-UPS," SAID THE SMALLEST BOY, BUT NO ONE LISTENED.

"HAVE YOU CONSIDERED HOW GRIM IT WOULD BE TO BE TIED UP ALL NIGHT?" THE FATTEST BOY SAID. "THIS BUSINESS OF MISSING ALL THE SPLENDID HALLOWEEN TREATS IS NO FUN."

THE SMALLEST BOY SAID, "IF YOU WERE ACQUAINTED WITH BOY SCOUT KNOTS, YOU COULD GET OUT OF THIS."

THIS TIME SOMEONE LISTENED. "OKAY, SMARTY. GET US OUT."

AND THE SMALLEST BOY DID.   114

COMPREHENSION: Record the student's retelling _____

_____

_____

WORD ACCURACY:

SUBSTITUTIONS   NUMBERS

Similar in sound
  (ex. — a, the /ə/,/ŏə/) .... _____ |_____ Underlined words missed
Similar in meaning |_____ .... Other words missed
  (ex. — big, large) .... _____ |_____ .... Total words missed
                                                |_____ ..... Perfect to 11 missed = Passed
                                                |_____ .... 12 or more missed = Failed

Test 32   SAN DIEGO ORAL PARAGRAPHS FORM I

Reader Level: Sixth

Note: Words underlined in the paragraphs are identical to those found on the San Diego
   Quick Assessment Form I.
PREREADING: Discuss pollution as a current problem; include ways to create a pollution-free
   environment.
Examiner: "READ THIS PARAGRAPH ALOUD. THINK ABOUT WHAT YOU ARE
   READING. THEN TELL ME IN YOUR OWN WORDS WHAT HAPPENED AND TO
   WHOM IT HAPPENED."

THE GIRLS WERE TOLD TO MAKE UP A NEW CITY IN A MAKE-
BELIEVE LAND BY USING ANY <u>APPARATUS</u>. THEY FLOATED A <u>BRIDGE</u>
ON A CUSHION OF AIR, AND IN THEIR LAND, A <u>TRUCKER</u> IS ABLE TO
CROSS A BRIDGE BY PUTTING UP A WIND SAIL. THE SAILS <u>ABOLISH</u>
POLLUTION FROM ALL CARS, AND <u>COMMERCIAL</u> FACTORIES HAVE
GIANT WIND MILLS FOR POWER. THE <u>NECESSITY</u> OF STORING WIND
FOR QUIET TIMES IS GREAT. A NEW IDEA ABOUT <u>RELATIVITY</u> WAS
FORMED. IT WAS NOT AS <u>ELEMENTARY</u> AS THE OLD IDEAS.

IN THE MAKE-BELIEVE LAND AN ART <u>GALLERY</u> IS MADE UP OF
MOVING FORMS. PEOPLE <u>COMMENT</u> ON THE BEAUTY OF MOTION. 106

COMPREHENSION: Record the student's retelling ＿＿＿＿＿＿＿＿＿＿

＿＿＿＿＿＿＿＿＿＿＿＿＿＿＿＿＿＿＿＿＿＿＿＿＿＿＿＿＿＿＿＿＿＿＿＿＿

＿＿＿＿＿＿＿＿＿＿＿＿＿＿＿＿＿＿＿＿＿＿＿＿＿＿＿＿＿＿＿＿＿＿＿＿＿

<u>WORD ACCURACY:</u>

SUBSTITUTIONS   NUMBERS

Similar in sound
   (ex. — a, the /ə/,/Ŏə/) .... _____ |_____ Underlined words missed
Similar in meaning |_____ .... Other words missed
   (ex. — big, large) .... _____ |_____ .... Total words missed
                                                 |_____ ..... Perfect to 10 missed = Passed
                                                 |_____ .... 11 or more missed = Failed

Test 32 SAN DIEGO ORAL PARAGRAPHS FORM I

Reader Level: Seventh

Note: Words underlined in the paragraphs are identical to those found on the San Diego Quick Assessment Form I.

PREREADING: Discuss the languages that are spoken in Canada. (French and British English)

Examiner: "READ THIS PARAGRAPH ALOUD. THINK ABOUT WHAT YOU ARE READING. THEN TELL ME IN YOUR OWN WORDS WHAT HAPPENED AND TO WHOM IT HAPPENED."

AMERICANS CELEBRATE THE FOURTH OF JULY, BUT CANADIANS CELEBRATE JULY FIRST. THEY CELEBRATE WHAT THEY CALL THE DOMINION OF CANADA DAY. THIS IS IN HONOR OF THE UNION OF CANADA UNDER ONE GOVERNMENT. THERE ARE TOO MANY PROVINCES IN THE DOMINION TO ENUMERATE THEM. DOMINIONS REMAIN LOYAL TO ENGLAND.

SOME CANADIANS SPEAK ENGLISH AND SOME SPEAK FRENCH. AMERICANS VISITING CANADA ARE DAUNTED BY THEIR OWN INABILITY TO SPEAK FRENCH WHEN THEY SEE VERY YOUNG CHILDREN SPEAKING THE LANGUAGE RAPIDLY. BOOKSTANDS ADVERTISE VARIOUS AND SUNDRY DICTIONARIES OF COMMON WORDS TO HELP WREST MEANING OUT OF WHAT IS HEARD. IMPETUOUS AMERICANS DARE TO TRY THEIR HIGH SCHOOL FRENCH ON SALES CLERKS WHILE SHY AMERICANS REMAIN QUIET.

SOME FRENCH WORDS ARE EASY TO LEARN. THE WORD FOR AMBER, THE YELLOWISH BROWN COLOR, IS "AMBRE" IN FRENCH. THE REASON THE WORDS ARE SO SIMILAR IS THAT AMBER COMES FROM THE FRENCH LANGUAGE. IN TRACING THE ORIGIN OF WORDS THERE IS MUCH BRANCHING OR CAPILLARY ACTION. SUCH WORDS AS AMBEROID, SYNTHETIC AMBER AND AMBERGRIS, USED IN PERFUME, ARE BRANCHES OF THE WORD AMBER.

TO GET BACK TO THE CANADIANS AND THEIR LANGUAGE, THE FRENCH-CANADIANS APPRECIATE HAVING VISITORS TRY TO SPEAK THEIR LANGUAGE. THEY CONSIDER IT A BLIGHT ON AMERICA THAT SO FEW AMERICANS CAN SPEAK MORE THAN ONE LANGUAGE. AS YOU SHOP IN A FRENCH-CANADIAN STORE THE CLERKS WILL CONDESCEND TO WAIT ON ENGLISH-SPEAKING CUSTOMERS. THEY GIVE MORE ATTENTION, HOWEVER, AS A USUAL PRACTICE, TO THOSE WHO MAKE AN ATTEMPT TO SPEAK THE NATIVE TONGUE. THEY ARE PLEASED WITH THOSE VISITORS WHO TRY TO EXPRESS THEMSELVES IN THE TONGUE OF THE COUNTRY THEY ARE VISITING.

COMPREHENSION: Record the student's retelling _____

_____

_____

WORD ACCURACY:

SUBSTITUTIONS   NUMBERS

Similar in sound
  (ex. — a, the /ə/,/ŏə/) .... ____ | ____ Underlined words missed
Similar in meaning | ____ .... Other words missed
  (ex. — big, large) .... ____ | ____ .... Total words missed
                                        | ____ ...... Perfect to 5 missed = Passed
                                        | ____ .... 6 or more missed = Failed

© 1978 by The Center for Applied Research in Education, Inc.

Test 32   SAN DIEGO ORAL PARAGRAPHS   FORM I

Reader Level: Eighth

Note: Words underlined in the paragraphs are identical to those found on the San Diego Quick Assessment Form I.

PREREADING: Discuss the desire of some people to build a monument to be remembered by.

Examiner: "READ THIS PARAGRAPH ALOUD. THINK ABOUT WHAT YOU ARE READING. THEN TELL ME IN YOUR OWN WORDS WHAT HAPPENED AND TO WHOM IT HAPPENED."

A LARGE BUILDING ROSE ABOVE THE ALREADY HIGH EMBANK-MENT. TO GIVE YOU SOME IDEA OF THE SIZE OF THE BUILDING YOU COULD SEE IT FROM FIVE MILES AWAY — WITHOUT BINOCULARS. SOME PEOPLE SAY THAT THE OWNER HAD DELUSIONS OF GRANDEUR. OTHERS SAY HE WANTED TO BECOME THE RICHEST MAN IN THE WORLD. HE BUILT WITH NO LIMITATIONS AS TO BUDGET. WHATEVER HIS PRETEXT WAS FOR BUILDING SUCH A HUGE BUILDING, EVERYONE AGREED IT WAS THE LARGEST IN ALL OF NORTH AMERICA.

EVERY DETAIL OF THE STRUCTURE AND GROUNDS WAS ELEGANT. THE ASCENT TO THE EMBANKMENT WAS BUILT WITH SPACIOUS STEPS. GARDENS AROUND THE BUILDING WERE IMMACULATE AND WELL KEPT. INSIDE THE ROOMS WERE CAPACIOUS WITH WIDE CORRIDORS AS WELL AS LARGE ROOMS. THE LIVING ROOM WAS LARGE ENOUGH FOR A FLEET OF CARS TO BE STORED.

HOW THE OWNER EVER AMASSED ENOUGH MONEY TO BUILD SUCH A STRUCTURE NO ONE WAS EVERY ABLE TO FIGURE OUT. LOTS OF TALK OF INTRIGUE SURROUNDED HIS LIFE, PARTICULARLY HIS FINANCES. PEOPLE WITH ACRID TONGUES SAID HE ROBBED BANKS. A MORE LOGICAL EXPLANATION WOULD BE THAT A RELATIVE HAD DIED LEAVING HIM A FORTUNE. BUT NO MATTER WHAT THE SOURCE, THE OWNER EVIDENTLY WANTED A MONUMENT THAT WOULD BE LONG ASSOCIATED WITH HIS NAME.

COMPREHENSION: Record the student's retelling _____

WORD ACCURACY:

SUBSTITUTIONS   NUMBERS

Similar in sound
 (ex. — a, the /ə/,/Ŏə/) .... _____ |_____ Underlined words missed
Similar in meaning |_____ .... Other words missed
 (ex. — big, large) .... _____ |_____ .... Total words missed
                                                |_____ ...... Perfect to 5 missed = Passed
                                                |_____ .... 6 or more missed = Failed

Cover Sheet

___

Test 33   *SAN DIEGO ORAL PARAGRAPHS* FORM II

Name _____ Grade _____   Chronological Age_____

                                                                        yr.   mo.

Date _____ Examiner _____   SDQA Reader Level.......... _____

Observations: _____   Minus 1 Grade Level........ _____

_____   Entry Oral ¶ Level.............. _____

_____   Ceiling Level .... _____

Materials: a. S.D. Oral Paragraph cards cut and collated so that the student sees only 1 card at a time. See Appendix IV.

               b. Copies of Student's Record Forms.

               c. Copy of student's performance on the SDQA.

PROCEDURE: 1. Record data on this Cover Sheet.

                  2. Read the prereading information on student record forms.

                  3. Record under word accuracy all of the words missed: mispronounced, omitted or substituted. Be sure to write in the substitutions as they sound to you by using diacritical marks or phonetic spelling.

WORDS MISSED at TOP level of the SDQA	WORDS MISSED AT the SAME level of Oral ¶	WORDS MISSED ON ORAL ¶ AT HIGHER LEVEL	WORDS MISSED ON ORAL ¶ AT LOWER LEVEL
_____	_____	_____	_____
_____	_____	_____	_____
_____	_____	_____	_____
_____	_____	_____	_____

✓ Check Appropriate Description:

_____ scored _____ grade level(s) higher on the SD Oral Paragraphs than on the SDQA, and therefore USES CONTEXT CLUES AS AN EFFECTIVE READING STRATEGY.

_____ scored _____ grade level(s) LOWER on the SD Oral Paragraphs than on the SDQA, which suggests an OVEREMPHASIS ON PHONICS.

_____ scored at the same grade level on the SD Oral Paragraphs as on the SDQA, which suggests that the STUDENT HAS REACHED HIS INTELLECTUAL CAPACITY OR THAT NOT ENOUGH EMPHASIS HAS BEEN PLACED ON MEANING. (Children, typically, score higher on paragraphs because context clues aid them.)

RECOMMENDATIONS: _____

_____

_____

_____

_____

Test 33   SAN DIEGO ORAL PARAGRAPHS FORM II

Reader Level: Preprimer

Note: Words underlined in the paragraphs are identical to those found on the San Diego Quick Assessment Form II.

PREREADING: If the students are unfamiliar with the rebus of the boy and girl heads as speakers, explain this to them.

Examiner: "READ THIS PARAGRAPH ALOUD. THINK ABOUT WHAT YOU ARE READING. THEN TELL ME IN YOUR OWN WORDS WHAT HAPPENED AND TO WHOM IT HAPPENED."

"COME HERE.

SEE.

'RIDE AND JUMP' IS MY BOOK."

I RAN TO SEE IT.

"IT IS RED.

IT LOOKS LIKE MY BOOK.

CAN IT BE MY BOOK?"

27

COMPREHENSION: Record the student's retelling _____

_____

_____

WORD ACCURACY:

SUBSTITUTIONS   NUMBERS

Similar in sound
  (ex. — a, the /ə/, /Ŏə/) .... _____ |—— Underlined words missed
Similar in meaning |———— .... Other words missed
  (ex. — big, large) .... _____ |———— .... Total words missed
                                                  |———— .... Perfect or missed 3
                                                  |———— .... Failed at 4 or more

Test 33   *SAN DIEGO ORAL PARAGRAPHS* FORM II

Reader Level: Primer

Note: Words underlined in the paragraphs are identical to those found on the San Diego Quick Assessment Form II.

PREREADING: Talk about books at school. What colors are they? Can any of them be taken home?

Examiner: "READ THIS PARAGRAPH ALOUD. THINK ABOUT WHAT YOU ARE READING. THEN TELL ME IN YOUR OWN WORDS WHAT HAPPENED AND TO WHOM IT HAPPENED."

"HE WANTS A BOOK.

IS THIS THE BOOK?"

"NO. IT WAS RED.

I WANT TO FIND ONE, TOO.

WE WILL TAKE THEM HOME.

WE LIKE BOOKS."

20

COMPREHENSION: Record the student's retelling _____

_____

_____

_____

_____

WORD ACCURACY:

SUBSTITUTIONS   NUMBERS

Similar in sound
  (ex. — a, the /ə/,/Ŏə/) .... _____ |—— Underlined words missed
Similar in meaning |—— .... Other words missed
  (ex. — big, large) .... _____ |—— .... Total words missed
                                            |—— .... Perfect or missed 3
                                            |—— .... Failed at 4 or more

Test 33   *SAN DIEGO ORAL PARAGRAPHS* FORM II

Reader Level: First

Note: Words underlined in the paragraphs are identical to those found on the
San Diego Quick Assessment Form II.

PREREADING: Have you played in the winter snow? Have you ever made snowballs?

Examiner: "READ THIS PARAGRAPH ALOUD. THINK ABOUT WHAT YOU ARE
READING. THEN TELL ME IN YOUR OWN WORDS WHAT HAPPENED AND TO
WHOM IT HAPPENED."

NOW IT IS WINTER. ALMOST ANY DAY THERE WILL BE LOTS

OF WHITE SNOW. MAYBE BY MONDAY WE WILL HAVE A LOAD

OF SNOW. I HOPE SO. LAST WINTER SNOW BANKS WERE HIGH.

FROM THE SNOW, I WILL MAKE TEN SNOWBALLS. I WILL

GIVE YOU FIVE. THEN LOOK OUT. I COULD SNOWBALL YOU.
                                                              53

COMPREHENSION: Record the student's retelling _____

_____

_____

_____

_____

WORD ACCURACY:

SUBSTITUTIONS   NUMBERS

Similar in sound
  (ex. — a, the /ə/,/ŏə/) .... _____ |_____ Underlined words missed
Similar in meaning |_____ .... Other words missed
  (ex. — big, large) .... _____ |_____ .... Total words missed
                                           |_____ .... Perfect or missed 5
                                           |_____ .... Failed at 6 or more

Test 33   *SAN DIEGO ORAL PARAGRAPHS* FORM II

Reader Level: Second

Note: Words underlined in the paragraphs are identical to those found on the San Diego Quick Assessment Form II.

PREREADING: Discuss the fact that sports performed on a track, such as running and jumping, are known as track sports.

Examiner: "READ THIS PARAGRAPH ALOUD. THINK ABOUT WHAT YOU ARE READING. THEN TELL ME IN YOUR OWN WORDS WHAT HAPPENED AND TO WHOM IT HAPPENED."

ANN WAS A FAST RUNNER. SHE WANTED TO BE ON THE TRACK TEAM. ONE DAY SHE FELL.

"SHE HURT HERSELF," ANOTHER GIRL SAID.

"NO, I DIDN'T," ANN SAID. SHE GOT UP BRAVELY.

"YOUR EAR IS DARK RED," HER FRIEND SAID. "YOU RECEIVED QUITE A BAD FALL."

"I'M OKAY," ANN SAID. "I WANT TO BE BACK AT SCHOOL FOR THE MAY DANCE."

"WE WILL SEE," SAID HER FRIEND.   67

COMPREHENSION: Record the student's retelling _____

_____

_____

WORD ACCURACY:

SUBSTITUTIONS   NUMBERS

Similar in sound
(ex. — a, the /ə/,/ŏə/) .... _____ |_____ Underlined words missed
Similar in meaning |_____ .... Other words missed
(ex. — big, large) .... _____ |_____ .... Total words missed
                                          |_____ .... Perfect or missed 7
                                          |_____ .... Failed at 8 or more

Test 33   SAN DIEGO ORAL PARAGRAPHS FORM II

Reader Level: Third

Note: Words underlined in the paragraphs are identical to those found on the San
Diego Quick Assessment Form II.

PREREADING: A riddle usually has a funny twist. Can you guess what tells time but cannot talk?
Yes, it is a clock.

Examiner: "READ THIS PARAGRAPH ALOUD. THINK ABOUT WHAT YOU ARE
READING. THEN TELL ME IN YOUR OWN WORDS WHAT HAPPENED AND TO
WHOM IT HAPPENED."

ONE BOY WENT TO <u>RECLAIM</u> HIS THIRD <u>GRADE</u> BOOK. HE

CAME BACK TO HIS <u>EIGHT</u> FRIENDS WHO WERE TELLING

<u>RIDDLES</u>. A <u>FEW</u> BOYS COULD NOT THINK OF ANY.

ONE BOY MADE A <u>MOVEMENT</u> AS IF TO GO.

"DON'T GO," THE OTHER BOYS SAID. "WE <u>ALREADY</u> HAVE A

GOOD ONE FOR YOU."

"WHAT MAKES YOU THINK OF A SKUNK? IT BEGINS WITH A

'C'. IT IS ANOTHER WAY OF SAYING PENNY."

"A <u>CENT</u>," ONE BOY SHOUTED ALL <u>ALONE</u>.

"OKAY, I GET IT. I SEE THE <u>LIGHT</u>," ANOTHER BOY SAID. 88

COMPREHENSION: Record the student's retelling _____

_____

_____

WORD ACCURACY:

SUBSTITUTIONS   NUMBERS

Similar in sound
    (ex. — a, the /ə/, /ŏə/) .... _____ |—— Underlined words missed
Similar in meaning |—— .... Other words missed
    (ex. — big, large) .... _____ |—— .... Total words missed
                                                     |—— .... Perfect or missed 9
                                                     |—— .... Failed at 10 or more

Test 33 *SAN DIEGO ORAL PARAGRAPHS* FORM II

Reader Level: Fourth

Note: Words underlined in the paragraphs are identical to those found on the San Diego Quick Assessment Form II.

PREREADING: Do scientists just work on helpful inventions? Discuss briefly.

Examiner: "READ THIS PARAGRAPH ALOUD. THINK ABOUT WHAT YOU ARE READING. THEN TELL ME IN YOUR OWN WORDS WHAT HAPPENED AND TO WHOM IT HAPPENED."

SCIENCE IS BECOMING MORE <u>IMPORTANT</u> THESE DAYS THAN IT USED TO BE. MANY SCIENTISTS <u>RESIDE</u> NEAR THEIR WORK. MANY NEW THINGS ARE <u>CENTERED</u> AROUND SCIENCE. PUSH BUTTON DIALING IS NEW. CHANGE IS <u>RETURNED</u> TO YOU IN STORES BY MACHINE. TV IS A <u>FAMOUS</u> INVENTION. SURELY WE LIVE IN A GREAT AGE.

SCIENCE THROWS US <u>CURVES</u> TOO. NOT ALL THAT IT DOES IS FOR OUR GOOD. IT INVENTS SOME <u>VIOLENT</u> THINGS, SUCH AS GUNS AND BOMBS. MANY OF THESE THINGS CAN BE USED IN THE <u>WRONG</u> WAY.   86

COMPREHENSION: Record the student's retelling _____

_____

_____

<u>WORD</u> <u>ACCURACY:</u>

SUBSTITUTIONS   NUMBERS

Similar in sound
  (ex. — a, the /ə/,/ŏe/) .... _____ |_____ Underlined words missed
Similar in meaning |_____ .... Other words missed
  (ex. — big, large) .... _____ |_____ .... Total words missed
                                          |_____ .... Perfect or missed 3
                                          |_____ .... Failed at 4 or more

Test 33 *SAN DIEGO ORAL PARAGRAPHS* FORM II

Reader Level: Fifth

Note: Words underlined in the paragraphs are identical to those found on the San Diego Quick Assessment Form II.

PREREADING: Can you tell me about a bicycle that you've fixed or that you've watched anyone else fix?

Examiner: "READ THIS PARAGRAPH ALOUD. THINK ABOUT WHAT YOU ARE READING. THEN TELL ME IN YOUR OWN WORDS WHAT HAPPENED AND TO WHOM IT HAPPENED."

I <u>ACQUIRED</u> A SECOND-HAND <u>BICYCLE</u> BUT THERE WAS TOO MUCH <u>INTERPLAY</u> BETWEEN THE PARTS. I HAD PLANNED TO RACE IT, BUT I WAS IN <u>DISTRESS</u>. THE WHEELS WOBBLED AND THE CHAINS BANGED. I FELT <u>DEFEATED</u>.

SHOULD I <u>CONSIDER</u> RESELLING IT? NO, I THOUGHT THAT I COULD PUT IT IN <u>SHAPE</u>. I WORKED HARD TO MAKE EVERYTHING FIT. THEN I POLISHED IT UNTIL IT SHONE IN A <u>BLAZE</u> OF <u>SPENDOR</u>. IT WAS BEAUTIFUL ENOUGH TO <u>ESCORT</u> THE WINNER OF A RACE.   80

COMPREHENSION: Record the student's retelling _____

_____

_____

<u>WORD</u> <u>ACCURACY</u>:

SUBSTITUTIONS   NUMBERS

Similar in sound
  (ex. — a, the /e/,/Ŏe/) .... _____ |_____ Underlined words missed
Similar in meaning |_____ .... Other words missed
  (ex. — big, large) .... _____ |_____ .... Total words missed
                                                |_____ .... Perfect or missed 8
                                                |_____ .... Failed at 9 or more

Test 33 SAN DIEGO ORAL PARAGRAPHS FORM II

Reader Level: Sixth

Note: Words underlined in the paragraphs are identical to those found on the San Diego Quick Assessment Form II.

PREREADING: Discuss banks and their need for security from within and without.

Examiner: "READ THIS PARAGRAPH ALOUD. THINK ABOUT WHAT YOU ARE READING. THEN TELL ME IN YOUR OWN WORDS WHAT HAPPENED AND TO WHOM IT HAPPENED."

BANKS AND LOAN CENTERS ARE <u>NOTABLE</u> BUILDINGS OF MARBLE AND POLISHED METALS. THEY ARE CONCERNED WITH <u>FINANCIAL</u> DEALINGS, <u>OPPOSITE</u> IN NATURE. BOTH ARE INTERESTED IN MONEY "TAKEN IN" AND IN MONEY "GOING OUT." BOTH NEED TIGHT <u>SECURITY</u>. BANK CLERKS WHO COMMIT A <u>BREACH</u> OF TRUST CAUSE BANKERS TO <u>LAMENT</u> AND TO GET MORE SECURITY. BANKS THAT ARE FREE OF ALL SUCH <u>CRIMES</u> ARE <u>LUCKY</u>. CRIMES OF <u>IGNORANCE</u> ARE FORGIVABLE BUT NOT THOSE OF THEFT. 75

COMPREHENSION: Record the student's retelling _____

_____

_____

WORD ACCURACY:

SUBSTITUTIONS   NUMBERS

Similar in sound
(ex. — a, the /ə/,/Ŏə/) .... _____ _____ Underlined words missed
Similar in meaning   _____ .... Other words missed
(ex. — big, large) .... _____ _____ .... Total words missed
                                              _____ .... Perfect or missed 7
                                              _____ .... Failed at 8 or more

© 1978 by The Center for Applied Research in Education, Inc.

189

Test 33   SAN DIEGO ORAL PARAGRAPHS FORM II

Reader Level: Seventh

Note: Words underlined in the paragraphs are identical to those found on the San Diego Quick Assessment Form II.

PREREADING: Discuss the problems of an author.

Examiner: "READ THIS PARAGRAPH ALOUD. THINK ABOUT WHAT YOU ARE READING. THEN TELL ME IN YOUR OWN WORDS WHAT HAPPENED AND TO WHOM IT HAPPENED."

THE WRITER WAS IN A <u>TORMENT</u>. IT WAS TWO YEARS SINCE HE HAD SOLD HIS LAST BOOK. HE HAD MADE NO <u>PROVISION</u> FOR SO LONG A TIME WITHOUT ANY INCOME. HE WAS A SMALL MAN WITH A <u>DAINTY</u> APPETITE BUT EVEN SO, HE WAS BEGINNING TO BE HUNGRY.

AS A YOUNG BOY HE HAD BEEN <u>AMBITIOUS</u>. HE WROTE WELL, AND WOULD WALK IN THE <u>MARSH</u> THINKING OF NEW STORIES. HIS MIND WOULD TAKE <u>FLIGHT</u> ESPECIALLY IN SPINNING TALES ABOUT <u>FRONTIER</u> DAYS. THEN HE WOULD <u>DESCEND</u> TO HIS BASEMENT DEN WHERE HE HAD A LARGE <u>STATIONARY</u> DESK. HE WOULD WRITE THERE UNTIL HIS <u>WRIST</u> ACHED.

COMPREHENSION: Record the student's retelling _____

_____

WORD ACCURACY:

SUBSTITUTIONS		NUMBERS

Similar in sound
 (ex. — a, the /ə/,/Ŏə/) .... ———— Underlined words missed
Similar in meaning .... Other words missed
  ....Total words missed
  ....Perfect or missed 10
  .... Failed at 11 or more

Test 33   *SAN DIEGO ORAL PARAGRAPHS* FORM II

Reader Level: Eighth
Note: Words underlined in the paragraphs are identical to those found on the San Diego Assessment Form II.
PREREADING: Discuss health diets briefly.
Examiner: "READ THIS PARAGRAPH ALOUD. THINK ABOUT WHAT YOU ARE READING, THEN TELL ME IN YOUR OWN WORDS WHAT HAPPENED AND TO WHOM IT HAPPENED."

NO TEACHER WOULD DEIGN TO TEACH HEALTH IN OUR SCHOOL

IN ANY ROOM BUT THE BIG GYMNASIUM. CONTRARY TO CONDITIONS

IN SOME SCHOOLS THE SUBJECT WAS ONE OF OUR MOST POPULAR.

OUR STUDENTS FLAUNTED THEIR KNOWLEDGE OF SUCH THINGS AS

DEFINITIONS OF PROTOPLASM, KINDS OF INSANITY, AND THE

IMPORTANCE OF GOOD NUTRITION. MOST CAME TO FEEL THAT DIET

IS THE GREAT SUN IN THE FIRMAMENT OF HEALTH, AND THEY BEGAN

TO SAVOR ALFALFA SPROUTS, AND ALL VEGETABLES AND FRUITS.

THEY EVEN, IN MANY CASES, PREFERRED THEM TO BISCUITS AND

PASTRIES.

COMPREHENSION: Record the student's retelling _____

_____

<u>WORD ACCURACY:</u>
SUBSTITUTIONS
Similar in sound
  (ex. — a, the /ə/,/ŏe/)
Similar in meaning
  (ex. — big, large)

NUMBERS

____ | ____ Underlined words missed
____ | ____ .... Other words missed
____ | ____ .... Total words missed
____ | ____ .... Perfect or missed 9
____ | ____ .... Failed at 10 or more

Test 34   TOPIC SENTENCES

Description: This test consists of 18 paragraphs (see pages 194-197). Each paragraph is preceded by basic ideas to alert the student as to content. Students are asked to select the topic sentences and place the numerals besides these sentences in the space provided.

Appropriate for: students who have difficulty concentrating, and also for those who tend to have low comprehension scores.

Ages: 8 to 16 (or grades 3^2 through 11)

Testing Time: 10 minutes.

Directions for Use:
1. Administer the test individually or to small groups.
2. Be sure the examples are marked correctly.
3. Try to establish a base level in which the student passes ALL three paragraphs.
4. The ceiling level is the highest level passed before the student fails; that is, a student passes a level if he correctly marks 2 out of 3 paragraphs.

Scoring the Test: Maximum score is 18 points. See the following key for answers to the test times.
Paragraphs 4, 7, 10, 13, 16 and 18 have the first and second sentences as the correct answers. If only one numeral is listed, the student is given half credit. Paragraph 11 is given full credit if the student's answer is *3* or if his answer is *3.4*. However, if 4 alone is marked, no credit is given.
Scores are plotted as follows:

	Grades	Expected Scores
Intermediate	3^2, 4, 5	1-6
Upper Grades	6, 7, 8	7-12
Secondary	9, 10, 11	13-18

Remediation: Select pages from activity books designed to teach topic sentences and/or main ideas. Have students underline topic sentences in paragraphs found in old children's magazines. As an extension of this same activity, have the students make up a short title to fit these paragraphs.

Answer Key

Paragraph Number	Topic Sentence Number	Paragraph ber Number	Topic Sentence Number
1	1	10	1,1
2	2	11	3,(4)
3	5	12	1
4	1,2	13	1,2
5	3	14	4
6	1	15	4
7	1,2	16	1,1
8	5	17	1
9	1	18	1,2

Test 34   TOPIC SENTENCES

Name _____ Grade _____   Chronological Age_____
                                                     yr.   mo.

Date _____ Examiner _____   Total Score_____
Observations: _____
_____

"Read one paragraph at a time. Immediately after this, select the topic sentence(s). Write the number(s) in the appropriate space."

Help the student to mark the examples correctly: A = 1   B = 2, 3.
(Read the paragraphs aloud IF necessary and explain the choices.)

EXAMPLES:

Paragraph Idea: drawing as a simple art

    A.   ¹You don't need many things to start drawing. ²A pencil, some paper and a scene of interest is enough. ³An eraser is sometimes used but you can and probably should get by without one. ⁴A few people like a drawing board, but it really isn't necessary.

                                                                     Ans._____

    B.   ¹To model with clay you need such things as sticks, knives, wire and water. ²Not so in drawing. ³Your needs are few. ⁴In fact, a pencil and paper are really all you need. ⁵Ceramics, oils, ink, pastels and almost any other art form requires cumbersome equipment.

                                                                     Ans._____

Test 34 (cont.)

"Read the following paragraphs silently and mark them as directed. Complete as many as you are able. If one paragraph seems too difficult, skip it and continue with the remaining paragraphs."

Paragraph Ideas: contest and Mary's jumping skill

1. [1]Mary can jump. [2]She can jump over a low wall. [3]She can jump rope. [4]And like a clown, she can jump and fall. [5]She never seems to get hurt. [6]She can jump as fast as a rabbit, too.

Ans._____

2. [1]Recess is a free play time. [2]During one recess the girls had a contest to see who could jump the highest. [3]Five of the girls jumped over 12 inches. [4]Six of them jumped about one and a half feet. [5]Mary was the last girl to try. [6]Everyone shouted. [7]Mary jumped three feet high. [8]The others could hardly believe their eyes.

Ans. _____

3. [1]Every day Mary practices. [2]At first she could scarcely jump one foot high. [3]Then she learned to lift her body. [4]Before she knew it, she could jump three feet high. [5]Mary now realizes the importance of daily practice in jumping.

Ans._____

Paragraph Ideas: Don's height and rapid growth

4. [1]Don is a tall five-year-old. [2]He is growing fast. [3]By the time he is ten, look out! [4]He may be tall enough to drop a ball in the basket.

Ans._____

5. [1]Don was a head taller than most of the boys in his class. [2]He was a few inches taller than most of the girls. [3]Without question he was the tallest boy in the fourth grade.

Ans._____

6. [1]Each year Don's mother put a mark on the door frame to show how tall he had grown. [2]She stopped adding any marks after his eighteenth birthday. [4]At this time he was as tall as his father. [5]His mother kept this record of growth to compare one year with another.

Ans. _____

Test 34 (cont.)

Paragraph Ideas: pretended and actual dislikes

7.　¹Sometimes boys act as though they dislike girls when they really do like them. ²Bill, however, really didn't like them. ³He had three sisters and they thought he was a pest. ⁴He thought they were monsters. ⁵They nagged him all day long: "Clean up your room. ⁶Put your skateboard away. ⁷Take out the garbage." ⁸They nagged and he didn't like it one bit. ⁹In fact, because of them he disliked girls. ¹⁰All girls.

Ans. _____

8.　¹Bill thought girls were bossy. ²Worst of all, you couldn't count on them to show up for practice on the baseball field; boys always show up. ³Girls never hit a home run; boys always hit at least a few. ⁴Girls never caught flies; boys almost always caught flies. ⁵Bill really didn't think girls were skilled in sports or dependable, and he really did not like them.

Ans. _____

9.　¹Bill didn't like girls. ²First of all he didn't like his oldest sister because she nagged him. ³He didn't like his middle sister because she made him dry the dishes. ⁴He didn't like his little sister because she broke his model planes. ⁵In fact, he couldn't think of a single girl he liked, but this was when he was 7 years old.

Ans. _____

Paragraph Idea(s): Pelé of Brazil and soccer's growing popularity in the United States

10.　¹Pelé is a famous soccer player from Brazil. ²He is helping soccer to gain in popularity in the United States. ³Many young boys wish they could play as well as Pelé. ⁴Soccer teams are being formed and the boys practice hard. ⁵Is there a team in your neighborhood yet? ⁶If not, I predict there will be one soon.

Ans. _____

11.　¹In playing soccer, only the goal keeper can stop the ball with his hands or arms. ²Each team uses 11 men to play. ³Many people in the United States are just learning facts like these about soccer because the sport is fairly new in our country. ⁴Before 1967 we did not even have professional teams here.

Ans._____

12.　¹Soccer is a sport that is very important to the South American countries. ²Brazil produced the top players in the world. ³Unlike South America, the United States has devoted little money and field space for soccer players. ⁴Professional teams did not even play here before 1967.

Ans. _____

Paragraph Ideas: Edison's inventions; the effect of his inventions.

13. ¹Edison lived to be eighty-four years old. ²During his lifetime he invented and patented twenty-five hundred items. ³Most of his time was spent on electricity and electrical items. ⁴Some important inventions of his were the phonograph, the electric light and motion pictures. ⁵So we have several reasons to be thankful that he was willing to devote his whole life to inventions.

Ans. _____

14. ¹Lighting our house is easy. ²Playing the phonograph is so simple that a child can do it. ³Motion pictures are enjoyed by most people. ⁴Have you ever thought that Edison gave us all these inventions and more?

Ans. _____

15. ¹How difficult life would be if we had to carry home kerosene for lamps. ²Dangerous it would be, too, because kerosene is explosive. ³How simple it is to snap a switch and have our rooms burst into light. ⁴In just this one electrical invention Edison took away danger and added comfort to our lives.

Ans. _____

Paragraph Ideas: 1848, gold in California

16. ¹In the early 19th century most of the population in this country was in the East. ²Something happened in the West to cause a population shift. ³Gold was discovered in California in 1848. ⁴Most people traveled west by wagon to get rich quick.

Ans. _____

17. ¹In 1948 gold was discovered in California and people began to travel west. ²Many people wanted to get rich fast. ³A few people did. ⁴Many others, however, worked hard but found no gold. ⁵Fortunes were made and lost in California.

Ans. _____

18. ¹In the early 19th century California had some Indians, a few missions, and very little else. ²In 1948 something happened to change this. ³A prospector discovered gold. ⁴When the news spread many people flocked to California to get rich quick. ⁵The land in California that was sparsely populated became crowded.

Ans. _____

Test 35   MODIFIED CLOZE

Description: This test includes items to test students beginning with the reading readiness level and proceeding through the eighth grade level (See pages 200-204). At the word or preprimer level, every fifth word was deleted and the student is to select a word to write in from the selection of words provided at the end of each level. Readability levels were extrapolated from Fry's Readability Scale.

This is a modified cloze technique since choices are provided. At the reading readiness level, every 7th letter has been deleted. At the preprimer through eighth-grade levels, every 5th word has been deleted.

Appropriate for: students who have learned to decode, have an adequate sight vocabulary, but have low comprehension scores.

Ages: 5 through 13, or older students with reading disabilities.

Testing Time: 10 minutes.

Directions for Use:
1. Administer the test individually, in small groups, or to a whole class.
2. Prereaders or readers at the preprimer or primer level should begin by working through the examples containing missing letters.
3. Students who read at the first reader level or above should work through at least 2 sentences on the chalkboard BEFORE beginning the test.

   Example: John is a boy. _____ is his very pretty _____

toy	sister	Robert	Mary

4. Inform students that *not* all of the words are needed to fill in the blanks.

Scoring the Test: Grade level standards for passing are shown in this chart:

Grade Level	Criterion for Passing
RR	*all* correct
Preprimer	no more than 1 error
Primer	no more than 1 error
First	no more than 1 error
Second	no more than 1 error
Third	no more than 1 error
Fourth	no more than 1 error
Fifth	no more than 2 errors
Sixth	no more than 2 errors
Seventh	no more than 2 errors
Eighth	no more than 2 errors

Remediation: Give students similar types of exercises to do while encouraging them to read ahead for meaning. Practice exercises of this kind can be made by selecting passages from basal readers in the classroom and deleting every 5th or 7th word. After the student fills in the blanks he or she can be directed to look up the original source to check the answers.

Answer Key

E   J   O
T   Z
g   n   u

Preprimer
can, and, play, me

Primer
the, big, man, back, yes, can

First
the, and, into, after,
little, shot, lions

Second
rode, liked, he, and, rock,
flipped, rode

Third
like, a, grown, big,
costs, like, out

Fourth
but, whales, you, mammals,
can, elephants, fish

Fifth
taught, they, to, their,
know, though, are

Sixth
are, copperheads, pit, have,
in, and, not, close, venom

Seventh
in, the, from, in, of, are,
and, their, a, of

Eighth
deal, by, and, words, rest,
leave, well-chosen, later,
fill

Test 35 MODIFIED CLOZE

Name _____ Grade _____ Chronological Age_____
                                                              yr.   mo.
Date _____ Examiner _____ Total Score _____
Observations:_____
_____
_____

Ages 5 and 6 begin here:

> "We will work through these missing letters together."
>
> A _____ C _____ E
> A B _____ D E _____ G H _____ J K
> "See if you can fill in these missing letters by yourself."
> Give the student help ONLY if he needs it.
>
> ABCD _ FGHI _ KLMN
>
> PQRS _ UVWX _ Z

"This time I cannot give you any help. See how well you can fill in the missing letters by yourself."

abcdef _ hijklm _ opqrst _ vwxyz

Children reading at the primary level may begin here. "Read the sentences and fill in the blanks with the words from below."

Preprimer

Look at me.
I _____ run and play.
Come _____ run with me.
Come _____ bat and ball with _____.
We can have some _____.

| can | and | me | fun | play | pay |

Test 35 (cont.)

Primer

The children looked at _____ fat fish. It was _____, very big.
"Can a _____ ride on the fish's _____?" a little boy asked.
"_____," said his Dad. "We _____ see him do this."

---

ride   can   man   big   back   yes   the

First

Five lions walked into _____ cage. They looked big _____ bold.
A man walked _____ the cage a minute _____ the lions. He looked _____ and scared.
Then he _____ a gun. Now the _____ looked scared.

---

little   opened   after   into   and   lions   the   shot

Test 35 (cont.)

Students reading at the intermediate level may begin here.

Second

The boy rode his ＿＿ with one hand. He ＿＿ to do tricks. Once ＿＿ did not watch carefully ＿＿ he ran over a ＿＿. Then his bicycle almost ＿＿ over. After that he ＿＿ using both hands.

---

rock	flipped	rode	liked	car	and	bicycle	he

Third

Lucky for those who ＿＿ watermelon but dislike seeds, ＿＿ seedless one has been ＿＿. It is not as ＿＿ a fruit. It also ＿＿ more. Most eaters will ＿＿ not having to spit ＿＿ the seeds.

---

big	out	costs	like	like	a	is	grown

Fourth

Elephants are large animals, ＿＿ would you believe that ＿＿ are even larger? Did ＿＿ know that whales are ＿＿ too? A baby whale ＿＿ weigh more than two ＿＿. And that is no ＿＿ story.

---

elephants	whales	but	me	you	can	fish	large	mammals

Test 35 (cont.)

Students reading at the upper grade level may begin here.

Fifth

Children in Thailand are _____ to respect their parents. _____ may want to go _____ a celebration but if _____ Dad says no, they _____ they cannot go. Even _____ they are disappointed they _____ expected to hide this.

---

are   their   they   taught   know   though   to   do

Sixth

Three snakes to avoid _____ rattlesnakes, water moccasins, and _____. These snakes are called _____ vipers which means they _____ a deep hollow pit _____ front of each eye _____ below it. You may _____ care to come that _____ to a reptile. Snake _____ can be fatal.

---

beware   have   and   close   venom   are   pit   in   not   copperheads

---

Seventh

To become a matador _____ Spain carried prestige. Often _____ art is passed on _____ father to son as _____ the story of Shadow _____ the Bull. Matadors who _____ outstanding become national heroes, _____ people admire them for _____ bravery. Very few give _____ thought to the plight _____ the bull.

---

of   in   from   because   their   are   in   the   of   a   is

---

Test 35 (cont.)

Eighth

Lincoln learned a great _____ about how to write _____ picking a well-written article _____ omitting appropriate and well-chosen _____. He would copy the _____ of the article but _____ blank spaces where the _____ words had been. Weeks _____ he would attempt to _____ in the missing words.

---

and   fill   deal   later   well-chosen   leave   by   words   rest

---

Test 36   MAZE/COMPREHENSION

Description: This test consists of 11 sets of paragraphs in which words have been replaced periodically by three alternatives, one of which is the correct word. (See pages 207-218.) From the first- through the fifth-grade levels, three choices have been substituted for every sixth word. At the sixth- through the tenth-grade levels, three choices have been provided for every sixth word after a 12-word running start.

The three-choice selection is made from two words that are the same part of speech and one word that is a different part of speech.

The readability of the 11 sets was extrapolated from Fry's Readability Scale.

Appropriate for: students who have difficulty comprehending and/or who are involved in a research program for the purpose of monitoring their progress.

Ages: 7 through 15, or older students with reading disabilities.

Testing Time: 10 minutes.

Directions for Use:
1. Administer the test to individuals, small groups, or a total class.
2. Follow the directions for presenting the example and subsequent paragraphs on the Cover Sheet, page 207.
3. Make sure that the example is understood.
4. Begin at the level on which you are sure the student will experience success. For example, if you have a seven-year-old who is reading at a preprimer or primer level, DO NOT ADMINISTER THIS TEST since the lowest reader level is the *First* Reader Level.
5. Encourage students to make a *choice* on each item until the reading becomes too difficult as indicated by a passage comprehension of 75% or less.

Scoring the Test: See the following key for answers to all paragraph sets.

Paragraphs 1-6

In paragraph sets for grades 1 through 6, the percentage is easily computed since the choices are based on 10. Eight correct choices is equal to 80% passage comprehension. Therefore, a score of 7 or less correct choices is considered a difficult passage level for the student to comprehend.

Paragraphs 7-10

In paragraph sets for grades 7 through 10, the ten correct choices are approximately 83% passage comprehension and can be considered easy for the student.

Number Correct	% Passage Comprehension	
1	08	
2	17	
3	25	
4	33	
5	42	FRUSTRATING
6	50	
7	58	
8	65	DIFFICULT
9	75	
10	83	
11	98	EASY
12	100	

Remediation: Read oral selections and pause before an obvious word to allow students time to write the word they anticipate. Immediately after this, read the correct word aloud. For example: "The fisherman put bait on a _____." (Hook is the correct word.)

Choose different parts of speech to delete to provide the student with varied practice.

Answer Key

1^2 name blackboard away on could all class boys got he

2^2 He before be he little slid The went began flew

3^1 shoe laces but on flip-flop of His He and as

3^2 checkers "Now more he After said jump where one a jumped

4 game to play takes ping-pong net ball the be bounce learn

5 is country player to team keep with except the who

6 you into of "how than sailing but into is wind

7 oxygen vacuum a could walking need carry systems are lift-off light system

8 earth and sun rays short causes white must path that and that

9 water balance the tank stand enough comfortable is Aquariums modern Chinese keep

10 solve experts to learn man's be been to as perform taught dolphin

Test 36   *MAZE/COMPREHENSION*   Cover Sheet

Name _____ Grade _____ Chronological Age_____

yr.   mo.

Date _____ Examiner _____ Starting Level _____

Observations: _____ Ceiling Level _____

_____

_____

"Read the following paragraphs silently. Whenever you come to a choice of 3 words, circle the word that you think makes the most sense.

"I will check the example you mark to be sure you understand how to mark this test."

```
Example:
                                        She
              I think kittens are nice. They are fun to
                                        But

              over
have in an  house.
        the

                              too
        I think dogs are about noisy.
                              work
```

"Continue marking the rest of the paragraphs in a similar manner. Work through as many as you are able."

Grade Level	% Pass	Correct * Part of Speech	In-correct		Grade Level	% Pass	Correct* Part of Speech	In-correct
First	_____	_____	_____		5th	_____	_____	_____
Second	_____	_____	_____		6th	_____	_____	_____
3¹	_____	_____	_____		7th	_____	_____	_____
3²	_____	_____	_____		8th	_____	_____	_____
4th	_____	_____	_____		9th	_____	_____	_____
					10th	_____	_____	_____

*But not a sensible substitution

RECOMMENDATIONS: _____

_____

_____

_____

_____

_____

_____

_____

1²

BOB GETS SOME HELP

                      nose.   blackboard.
Bob could not see his name. It was written on the girl.   But it was too
                      was.   into.

     very   on
far gone His teacher put many words inside the blackboard. Poor Bob! He
   away.   have

hardly
would not see any of them!
could

   Sure   class   boys
  All   of the girls in his country could read. Most of the kittens could read,
  None   pretty   went

too.

            come   it
Then Bob tall   a pair of glasses. Now over can read.
         got   he

Level of Passage Comprehension _____%

Test 36 (cont.)

2²

BOB LEARNS TO SKI

               He   because.
Bob put on his skis. She had never had skis on during. He wondered if he
              The   before.

        be   on   but
would have able to stand up as it tried to go down a little hill. The first time he
      onto   he   husky

slid   An   white
swam down the hill standing up. The next hill was bigger. He went so very fast
great   The   wrote

       before   truly
that he began to fall and his skis melted over his head.
      painted   flew

Level of Passage Comprehension _____%

© 1978 by The Center for Applied Research in Education, Inc.

3[1]

BOB LEARNS TO ICE SKATE

           but   and
Bob laced up his high scarf skates. He pulled up the laces   as tight as he
             shoe   shutters

       but   softly   flip-flop.
could, butter the minute he coasted out under the ice his ankles went quietly.
     and   on   into.

               color   His
The ice scraped the inside after his ankle, then the outside. Her legs felt weak
               of   Place

         Where   but
like spaghetti. He   coasted back to the bench and sat down. Skating was
          It   neat

    like
not under easy as it looked.
    as

Level of Passage Comprehension _____%

Test 36 (cont.)
3²

BOB LEARNS TO PLAY CHECKERS

                          diving   "House
Bob's dad took out the checkers and set up the checkerboard. "How the
                          mice   "Now

                    an   he
point is to take more of your partner's checkers than it takes of yours," he
                  none   quite

explained.

Under   sailed   jump
Going a few moves, Bob's dad said , "Now Bob, you need to over me."
After   silly   ride

              where   beside
Bob had to ask white and after that he took one of his dad's men. Then
               very   fire

more   hope
an   catastrophe happened as his dad jumped all three of his men.
a   sailed

Level of Passage Comprehension _____%

© 1978 by The Center for Applied Research in Education, Inc.

Test 36 (cont.)

4

PLAYING PING-PONG

           throw   to play
Ping-pong is not a difficult game ; in fact, most people learn to run easily
           cave   to her

         where   ping-pong
and well. All it wants is two wooden paddles, a kitchen table, ping-pong
         takes   hitting

     rosy.
balls and a net.
     needle.

                  ball   run
The server must get the barber over the net and in the right court. The ball
                 come   an

   red   bounce   school
must am returned so that it will jump on the table. Players must skip to
   be   couch   learn

move fast.

Level of Passage Comprehension ⎯⎯⎯⎯%

© 1978 by The Center for Applied Research in Education, Inc.

212

PLAYING SOCCER

Soccer is a game that is $\genfrac{}{}{0pt}{}{down}{was}$ becoming more popular in this $\genfrac{}{}{0pt}{}{going.}{vase.}$ $\genfrac{}{}{0pt}{}{}{country.}$ Pelé who is a famous

$\genfrac{}{}{0pt}{}{player}{judge}{handsome}$ from Brazil has helped $\genfrac{}{}{0pt}{}{too}{to}{in}$ interest us in the sport.

Each $\genfrac{}{}{0pt}{}{were}{herd}{team}$ uses eleven men and they $\genfrac{}{}{0pt}{}{keep}{kite}{close}$ the ball on the move with $\genfrac{}{}{0pt}{}{think}{behind}$ any part of their

body except their hands. The goalkeeper is an $\genfrac{}{}{0pt}{}{unless}{boys}$ one $\genfrac{}{}{0pt}{}{go}{the}$ man on the team who $\genfrac{}{}{0pt}{}{needs}{what}$ can touch the ball

with his hands.

Level of Passage Comprehension _____%

Test 36 (cont.)

MODERN SAILING

you
Modern sailing is no longer a simple task as anyone will tell her who has attempted to sail
how

speedy   racing   "how
into   the wind. It takes knowledge near "what to do," practice in "doubtless to do it,"
over   of   "beautiful

than
and more and   a little skill.
courage

color   into   when
"Running" or sailing with the wind is easy than not as fast as sailing into   the wind or
washing   but   between

"tacking."

at   where
"Trimming" is   a way of directing the wind so that it fills out the sail.
are   tree

Level of Passage Comprehension _____%

7   Running Start of 12 Words

ASTRONAUTS TAKE OFF

typing

An astronaut space suit is very bulky because it houses supplies of oxygen   and protects

television

vacuum   tiny   fast

the wearer from the virtues of space in case of an   breakdown in air pressure which could

beside   a   had

occur in the spacecraft.

kindly   need   working

For dancing on the moon, the men camp even more protection. They must cattle   a

walking   neat   carry

systems   are

backpack with portable life-support wisely   and emergency oxygen. Space suits not worn

garages   was

dangerous.   nude

as a safeguard during lift-off.   Astronauts usually fly in washing flight overalls.

sit-downs.   light

underneath

The rocket's guidance system   controls the engines that lift and steer the ship.

hook

Level of Passage Comprehension _____%

Test 36 (cont.)

8 Running Start of 12 Words

A RED SUNSET

transports
The atmosphere is like a huge circular protective blanket. It surrounds the earth
universe

and   sun
and scatters the sun's blue than   violet light rays. When the winter   is directly
purple   penetrating

far   darkly
overhead the light glue have a relatively direct and short   trip through the atmosphere.
rays   lonesome

moisture   white.   play
This causes   the sun to appear almost wanting. At sunset the light rays must follow
crates   fretful.   quite

closet   that
an oblique and longer choose and consequently, we can say certainly the position of
path   which

on   went
the earth and its atmosphere influences the color they the sun appears to be.
than   that

Level of Passage Comprehension _____%

Test 36 (cont.)

AQUARIUMS

An unusual and attractive aquarium is a round sealed tank full of his   which is

(above "his": water)   (below "his": soil)

equipped with a beyond of sea life so that the bowl remains clean. This unusual

(above "beyond": child) (below "beyond": balance)   (above "the": after) (below "the": an)

tank is built onto a silver searching which provides light and heat enough to keep the

(above "tank": building) (below "tank": underscore) (above "searching": stand) (below "searching": whirlpool) (above "enough": plunged) (below "enough": shapely)

tropical fish narrate and while the total unit am impressive — it is shockingly

(above "narrate": noisy) (below "narrate": comfortable) (above "am": is) (below "am": overcast)

expensive!

Aquariums are far from being a lignite device. In ancient times the Martians were

(above "Aquariums": Afterward) (below "Aquariums": Aquarius) (above "lignite": usable) (below "lignite": modern) (above "Martians": Chinese) (below "Martians": liberal)

probably the first to arrive fish in containers indoors.

(above "arrive": keep) (below "arrive": lordly)

Level of Passage Comprehension _____%

INTELLIGENCE OF ANIMALS

Scientists measure intelligence by observing the behavior of animals when attempting to

solve
underneath a problem.
destroy

                  vicar   to   normal.
According to some herewith apes and monkeys are next in man in their ability to sleep.
              experts   go   learn.

                     man's   tacit
Dolphins have brains much like amoebas— what's more, they appear to is   protective of
                    fighting   be

           lanky   be
man and have been known to guide shipwreck survivors to shore. Places of entertainment
           gone   at

    as   perform   taught
such ever   Sea World train Dolphins to graduate amazing tricks. Whales can be often
   pretty   grit   spanked

                  pamper
stunts, too, but the bottle-nosed dolphin is the smartest animal in the ocean.
                  goldfish

Level of Passage Comprehension _____%

Test 37 QUALITY OF COMPREHENSION

Description: This test consists of a short episode written at reader level one, as extrapolated from Fry's Readability Scale. (See page 222.) The test measures comprehension at three levels:
1. Quantity (number of facts recalled regardless of order)
2. Organization (main idea and characters)
3. Quality (inferential and extended)

Appropriate for: students who have difficulty in answering questions at the end of a reading lesson.

Ages: 6 through 9 (Grades 1² through Grade 4), or older students with reading difficulties.

Testing Time: 5 minutes.

Directions for Use:
1. Administer the test individually.
2. First ask the student to read the selection aloud from the copy found on page 222.
3. Mark *S O* over the words that are *sounded out* on the examiner's copy or Cover Sheet, page 221.
4. If, after 5 seconds, the student is unable to sound out the word, say it and put a line underneath the word.
5. Allow the child to study the copy for 6 seconds before asking for recall of what was read.
6. Next, ask the main event and who the story is about.
7. Ask the Bonus Question, if necessary.
8. The second time through, read aloud the total selection while the student listens.
9. Proceed in the same sequence as above for the total recall and questioning.

Scoring the Test: The test yields 12 scores — 7 after the student reads aloud, and 5 after the teacher reads aloud.

The total recall after the first reading should be:

Minimum %

$1^2 = 50\%$
$2^2 = 60\%$
$3^2 = 70\%$
$4^2 = 80\%$

Total recall after the examiner's reading aloud should be:

$1^2 = 60\%$
$2^2 = 70\%$
$3^2 = 80\%$
$4^2 = 90\%$

All of the listening scores should be higher than the reading aloud scores since this is the student's second exposure to both a visual and auditory exercise.

Remediation: In those instances where the listening scores are lower, additional testing in the area of auditory perception should be given. One such test is the Lindamood LAC test.

In cases where there is no hearing impairment, the student should be given tasks similar to the test situation. For this purpose, paragraphs may be taken from a basal reader.

Cover Sheet

Test 37   QUALITY OF COMPREHENSION

Name _____ Grade_____
Date _____ Examiner _____
Observations:_____
_____
_____

Chronological Age_____
Percentage of Total Recall

1 = 5%	7 = 35%	14 = 70%
2 = 10%	8 = 40%	15 = 75%
3 = 15%	9 = 45%	16 = 80%
4 = 20%	10 = 50%	17 = 85%
5 = 25%	11 = 55%	18 = 90%
6 = 30%	12 = 60%	19 = 95%
	13 = 65%	20 = 100%

Total Recall Facts

____1   A boy went out.
____2   He walked
____3   down the street.
____4   The sun
____5   was just coming up.
____6   All at once,
____7   he saw something.
____8   "It shines,"
____9   he said.
____10 "Maybe it's diamonds."

____11 He walked closer.
____12 "It's NOT diamonds.
____13 It shines like silver.
____14 It is a purse, and
____15 I will get it.
____16 Maybe it has money."
____17 He tried to pick it up.
____18 But all at once, it slid away.
____19 It slid into the bushes.
____20 Someone in the bushes laughed.

READING SCORES	*LISTENING SCORES*	*DIFFERENCE*
Words sounded out _____		
Pronounced by examiner_____		
Total recall % _____	_____	_____
Who is the story about?_____	_____	_____
What happened? _____	_____	_____
Bonus questions:		
Can you figure out what		
time of day it was? _____	_____	_____
Why did the purse		
disappear? _____	_____	_____

In the first bonus question you are searching for the observation that the sun rises in the morning and therefore the boy was up early. If this information is given as he recalls the content there is NO need to question him. Just be sure to give credit for it.

In the second bonus question you are searching for some recognition that the purse did not vanish of its own accord, and recognition that someone masterminded the prank, joke or trick. This, too, may have been included in the total recall and if so should not be re-questioned.

Test 37   QUALITY OF COMPREHENSION

"This story is entitled *Something Shiny*. Please read it aloud to me but *think* about what you are reading because after you have finished reading it I want you to tell me as much as you can remember about it."

A boy went out. He walked down the street. The sun was just coming up. All at once, he saw something.

"It shines," he said. "Maybe it's diamonds."

He walked closer. "It's not diamonds. It shines like silver. It is a purse, and I will get it. Maybe it has money."

He tried to pick it up. But all at once, it slid away. It slid into the bushes. Someone in the bushes laughed.

Allow the student 6 seconds to look over the story. Then take this copy away and say, "Tell me as much about what you read as you can remember."

Section VII Summary

In summary, all of the tests in this section are concerned with comprehension rather than vocabulary knowledge. For this reason the vocabulary is kept simple or the student is prepared for it through a prereading introduction. In the case of the Quality of Comprehension Test, which is read orally by the student, any word too difficult for the student to sound out is supplied.

References

Blachowicz, Camille, "Cloze Activities for Primary Readers," *The Reading Teacher,* Dec. 1977, 31, 300-302.

——————, "Semantic Constructivity in Children's Comprehension," *Reading Research Quarterly,* XIII, No. 2, 1977-1978, 188-199.

Fry, Edward, "A Reading Formula That Saves Time," *Journal of Reading,* Apr. 1968, 163-164.

——————, "The Readability Graph Validated at Primary Levels," *The Reading Teacher,* Mar. 1969, 22, No. 6, 534-538.

SECTION VIII

assessing affective measures

(Contains Tests 38-42)

Interest Measures

Teachers need some measure of students' interests to assist them in selecting books, as well as in expanding their reading horizons. Most measures of interests are those directly gathered from the students themselves, and even these change over a period of time.

A fifth grader who is interested in reading only about football can be encouraged to branch out to other sports, from sports to the Olympics, and from the Olympics to the countries that have hosted these contests, ad infinitum. A note of caution is appropriate. Not all students should be dealt with in this manner.

Occasionally, students display an interest early in life which, when pursued through books, a lifetime of experience and practice, allows them to excel in their chosen field. Edison was an example of such a person. Had an adult tried and succeeded in dislodging his interest from the field of science, the course of history could well have been different.

In addition to specific individual interests, students typically have interests as follows:

Primary children —	pets, animal stories, picture books
3rd/4th graders —	horses, dogs, and other animals Indians, riddle books
5th/6th graders —	fairy tales, adventures, fables, humorous stories, joke books
7th/9th graders —	adventure stories, mysteries, success stories, myths
10th/12th graders —	science fiction, biography, mysteries, romance, historical novels, sports

Beyond these typical choices, the best method of assessing individual interests is to observe students as they browse in the library, looking, touching, and sampling the writing of books that appeal to them. However, this method is not always practical. There are times when a teacher does not have a well-stocked library; and there are times when she needs comprehensive information about the unique interests of her total class to be able to order books from a central source. For such times, it helps to administer a simple interest inventory such as any of those presented in this section of the *File*.

Attitude Measures

Attitudes toward reading are best measured by direct observation. Such specific measures as a parent's observation of his child's spending two out of five after-school hours in reading-related activities is a stronger indication that the child likes reading than the child's statement that he spends "some" time reading after school.

Attitude changes are effected slowly, yet they are of paramount importance in bringing about progress in reading achievement. A negative attitude toward reading leads to avoidance. Avoidance leads to disuse. While disuse may not lead to complete extinction, it comes dangerously close. Pre- and post-measures of attitudes can be as revealing as pre- and post-measurements of reading achievement, and ought to be included as a vital part of reading research.

Inventory Overview

Table IX provides a brief overview of the interest and attitude measures included in this section.

Table IX

Inventory Guide 38-42

Test	Title	Ages	Minutes	Appropriate for:
38	Primary Interest Inventory	5-7	3	students not motivated to read
39	Intermediate Interest Inventory	8-9	10	students not motivated to read
40	Upper Grade Interest Inventory	10-17	6	students not motivated to read
41	Primary Attitude Measure	5-7	10	students having difficulty learning to read
42	Self-Anchoring Attitude Scale	6-20	5	students to monitor attitude changes

Test 38 PRIMARY INTEREST INVENTORY

Description: For this assessment you will need three index cards, each containing a different facial expression, and a copy of the Cover Sheet on page 228 to record each student's responses:

Appropriate for: classes or individuals for whom an interest inventory is needed.

Ages: 5-7 or from kindergarten through grade 2.

Time: 3 minutes per child.

Directions for Use:

As preparation for giving the inventory, be sure to explain to the class that there are no right or wrong answers — just answers that tell us how they feel about certain kinds of books. Discuss the importance of HONEST answers with the whole class so that it will not be necessary to spend time with each child explaining its importance.

NOTE: It is essential to establish likes and dislikes before administering the inventory or you are unlikely to get HONEST answers.

Administer the inventory individually, following the directions on the Cover Sheet, page 228. Read each of the items aloud to the child and ask him or her to point to the card with the facial expression that best conveys the true feelings about the item: happy, so-so, or unhappy.

The examples given are to establish different responses from the child. These may be extended IF necessary.

Scoring: When you have finished giving the inventory to each child, use a Cover Sheet blank to tabulate all of the responses in the group or class.

Cover Sheet

Test 38   PRIMARY INTEREST INVENTORY

Name _____ Grade _____   Chronological Age _____

Date _____ Examiner _____   Circle the no. of 😊 responses

Observations: _____

	1 ____ 5 ____ 9 ____
	2 ____ 6 ____ 10 ____
	3 ____ 7 ____ 11 ____
	4 ____ 8 ____ 12 ____

Teacher:

"I need to order some books for use in our classroom. Please help me pick out books that you will like.

Here are 3 cards. One has a very happy face. One has an everyday face. And one has a very unhappy face. As I read each sentence about these books, or about your feelings in general, please point to the card which expresses your feelings. We will work through these three examples to make sure you know what is expected of you in this task."

EXAMPLE

Sentences:

How do you feel about:

	😊	😐	🙁
a. — eating a large ice cream cone? _____			
b. — taking out the trash? _____			
c. — drinking milk? _____			

Interest Inventory

1. — stories of pets like cats, dogs, parrots or goldfish? _____			
2. — animal stories such as Peter Rabbit, Winnie the Pooh, and Snoopy? _____			
3. — books that have lots of good pictures and hardly any writing? _____			
4. — stories that make you laugh? _____			
5. — stories that are sad? _____			
6. — stories that have lots of people in them? _____			
7. — stories about airplanes, trains, and trucks? _____			
8. — stories of rockets and space travel? _____			
9. — books that tell you how to cook? _____			
10. — books with funny pictures? _____			
11. — books that tell how to make things? _____			
12. — books about boys and girls? _____			

Test 39 INTERMEDIATE LEVEL INTEREST INVENTORY

Like primary level students, students at the intermediate level show their interest best by selecting from books in a well-stocked library. However, for teachers who need to order books from lists, catalogs, or a central source, student inventories given periodically are a help. At this level students can mark their preferences on their own papers, in small groups, or in an inventory given to the whole class.

As in the case of the primary class, an essential step is to make sure that the whole class understands the importance of honesty in their responses.

Description: This inventory consists of ten story topics and a five-choice level of feeling response (page 230):

strongly like    not as strongly like   so-so   don't like   hate

Appropriate for: intermediate students for whom an assessment of interests is needed.

Ages: 8 and 9, or students in grades 3 and 4.

Time: 10 minutes for the whole class.

Directions for Use:

To prepare for the inventory, be sure to establish rapport with the class and explain the necessity for honest answers. Tell the class that there are no right or wrong answers — only answers that show how they feel about certain kinds of books.

Administer the inventory to the entire class, providing each student with an individual copy (page 230).

Scoring: Use a blank copy of the inventory to tabulate the number of students who strongly like (column 5) and who not so strongly like (column 4) any one type of book.

Test 39 INTERMEDIATE INTEREST INVENTORY

Name _____ Grade _____   Chronological Age _____
Date _____ Examiner _____   Tabulation of response:

Observations: _____

1 _____ 6 _____
2 _____ 7 _____
3 _____ 8 _____
4 _____ 9 _____
5 _____ 10 _____

If you strongly like a statement put an X in column 5; if not as strongly put an X in 4; if you feel just "so-so" put an X in column 3; if you do not like a statement put an X in 2; if you thoroughly dislike or even hate the subject, put an X in column 1.

	Col. 5	Col. 4	Col. 3	Col. 2	Col. 1
EXAMPLE: How do you feel about:					
—playing a game with your best friend?					
—staying at home with a broken leg in a cast?					
—cleaning up your room?					
1. —stories about horses?					
2. —stories about dogs?					
3. —stories about animals?					
4. —stories about Indians?					
5. —riddle books?					
6. —funny stories?					
7. —history, or pioneer-day stories such as The Little House on the Prairie?					
8. —sad stories such as Charlotte's Web?					
9. —detectives like Encyclopedia Brown?					
10. —adventure stories like Boxcar Children?					

Test 40 UPPER GRADE INTEREST INVENTORY

Upper grade and secondary students have a wider spread of books from which to choose. Gifted students, for example, have interests and abilities that permit them to enjoy books written for young adults. The average child in the upper grades also has a greater stock of subjects from which to make his choices. An inventory at this level therefore includes categories that are broad, such as domestic animals rather than pets.

Description: This inventory of interests (page 232) lists 18 types of books or stories and provides five response-choices for each, ranging from "Never choose" to "Usually choose."

Appropriate for: upper grade and secondary students for whom an interest inventory is needed.

Ages: 10-17 or grades 5 through 12.

Time: 6 minutes.

Directions for Use:

Administer the inventory to the entire class, providing each student with a copy (page 232). Be sure to establish rapport and point out the necessity of giving honest answers.

Scoring: Use one of the inventory sheets to tabulate the responses of the class.

Test 40   UPPER GRADE INTEREST INVENTORY

Name _____ Grade _____   Chronological Age _____
Date _____ Examiner _____   Tabulation Responses _____
Observations: _____   1 __ 5 ___ 9 __ 13 __ 17__
_____   2 __ 6 __ 10 __ 14 __ 18 __
_____   3 __ 7 __ 11 __ 15 __
                                    4 __ 8 __ 12 __ 16 __

Place an X in the column that best describes which books you would choose.

Books I would choose	Never	Seldom	Maybe	Sometimes	Usually	
stories about domestic animals						
wild animal stories						
mysteries and detective stories						
romance						
high adventure						
fantasy stories						
science fiction						
"how to" books						
books of humor, jokes, riddles						
books on magic						
humorous stories						
short stories						
historical novels						
biographies						
western stories, cowboys, etc.						
camping and backpacking						
music, arts and crafts						
sports books						

Test 41   PRIMARY ATTITUDE MEASURE

Description: This measure (page 235) consists of 16 statements of a student's behavior as observed by a parent.

Appropriate for: students in the primary grades.

Ages: 5-7 or kindergarten through grade 2.

Time: 10 minutes.

Directions for Use:

Give a copy of the attitude measure (page 235) to the child's parent and ask that the items be checked directly. Or, you may gather the information yourself in an interview with the parent.

Scoring: Data of this kind should be stored, reassessed at a later date, and the findings compared. In those instances in which teachers note a *negative* difference, some steps need to be taken to improve the student's attitude and, if possible, to eliminate factors which caused the negative change.

In recording this information note that ALL of the even items 2-16 plus items 3 and 7 are associated with children having a *good* attitude toward learning and reading. Children checked in these areas are interested in letters, words, and stories. They are reflective and therefore enjoy looking closely at detail, shapes and forms before responding. They prefer to be correct on their first try. Reading is a fairly exacting skill and like the form of a puzzle piece both letters and words need to be carefully scrutinized.

Supplemental Observations: Six observations that are easy for the teacher to record at school and that supplement the parent's record provide further measurements of the child's behavior:

Based on a week's observation —

1. When the teacher reads a story aloud in class:

    _____ total attention
    _____ 60% attention
    _____ easily distracted

2. When another student reads aloud to the class:

    _____ total attention
    _____ 60% attention
    _____ easily distracted

3. During class library periods:

    _____ reads most of the period
    _____ reads half of the period
    _____ flips pages

4. During free-choice periods:

_____ chooses reading 50% or more of the time
_____ seldom chooses reading
_____ never chooses reading

5. When asked to volunteer to read aloud to a small group:

_____ often volunteers
_____ seldom volunteers
_____ never volunteers

6. During silent reading:

_____ completes assignments
_____ seldom completes assignments
_____ never completes assignments

Test 41 PRIMARY ATTITUDE MEASURE

Name _____ Grade _____ Chronological Age _____
Date _____ Parent_____

Please put a ✓ in front of each statement that describes your child's behavior.

___1 prefers to be active rather than to listen to stories being read to him.

___2 asks for help with reading and writing.

___3 (if kindergarten age) is able to write his name.
      (if grade one) can write a sentence without help.
      (if grade two) can write a sentence longer than four words.

___4 (since child was able to hold book) has always loved to turn pages and look at books.

___5 loves to play hide and seek and other outdoor games.

___6 asks about letters and words on cereal boxes and billboards.

___7 chooses to listen to records.

___8 (at preschool age) pretended to read stories by telling about the pictures.

___9 would only listen to stories before falling asleep at night.

__10 (as a kindergarten child) he began to notice parts of his favorite story were omitted.

__11 prefers running, skipping, and jumping, to small-muscle activities like putting an 8-piece puzzle together.

__12 memorized almost totally a story often reread to him.

__13 "impulsive" in actions; that is, the child would quickly place a puzzle piece in several incorrect places and not mind that they were not the same shape.

__14 "reflective" in thinking; that is, the child would hold a puzzle piece and study it carefully before selecting the correct space for it.

__15 relaxes in front of the TV after school.

__16 watches no more than one TV program on school nights.

Test 42   SELF-ANCHORING ATTITUDE SCALE

Description: This is a wide-range attitude scale (page 238); that is, it can be used in research with kindergarten through college age students. Furthermore, the scale can be used with a student who would choose to do any odious task rather than read, as well as with students who would rather read than eat. Like all affective measures the scale is only as valid as the honesty of the student's response.

Appropriate for: (1) use in research studies in which pre- and post-measures of attitudes are needed; (2) discovering differences in how students value reading; and (3) assessing the way a student perceives his own attitude toward reading when compared with others.

Ages: 6-20 or grade 1 through college.

Time: 5 minutes.

Directions for Use:

Administer the scale to individuals, to small groups of students, or to the total class of mature students. At the primary level, give the scale on an individual basis, writing in the answers as the child works through it. Alter the directions for students old enough to write in their own choices and descriptive phrases.

Follow this procedure with young children:

1. Show the child a copy of the scale (page 238) numbered from 10 through 0.
2. Say, "Name someone you know who LOVES to read." (Write the name in after number 10.)
3. Say, "Name someone you know who HATES reading." (Write the name in after 0.)
4. Explain that number 5 stands for the AVERAGE readers in your class.
5. Ask the student to imagine that ALL of the in-between numbers describe readers somewhere on the ladder from Loves to Hates.
6. Ask the student to select a rank in number. (If he already thinks of himself as a 10 or 0, skip this question. Otherwise, write in the student's name as directed.)
7. Next ask the student what _____, who is number 10, does to show a LOVE for reading. (Write the child's descriptive phrases.)
8. Ask the student what _____, who is number 0, does to show a HATRED for reading. (Write the child's descriptive phrases.)

Scoring: Comparisons of the self-anchoring descriptions will supply the teacher with insights into the value students place on reading. Here are some examples taken from three fourth-grade students' papers:

> 10 My dad
>
> because he reads the newspaper every night.
>
> 10 My mom
>
> because she's always reading a magazine when I get home from school.
>
> 10 My aunt
>
> because she's a librarian and she says she'd rather read than eat.

Of the three persons mentioned, it seems obvious that the aunt who would rather read than eat is the only one who loves to read. Reading the daily newspaper or a weekly magazine is better than not reading at all but it places an average value on reading.

We know that children are influenced by people around them who place a value on reading. For this reason it helps to know who the child perceives as having a real liking for reading. The reverse is equally true. Children raised in an environment where no one places value on reading are most likely to dismiss reading as unimportant.

Test 42 SELF-ANCHORING ATTITUDE SCALE

Name _____ Grade _____ Chronological Age _____
Date _____ Teacher _____ Pretest _____ Posttest ____
                                                  Gain _____ Loss _____

Pretest   Posttest   Date _____

10 name: _____   10 name: _____
   because: _____   because: _____
   _____   _____
   _____   _____
   _____   _____
   _____   _____
   _____   _____

9 _____   9 _____
8 _____   8 _____
7 _____   7 _____
6 _____   6 _____
5 _____   5 _____
4 _____   4 _____
3 _____   3 _____
2 _____   2 _____
1 _____   1 _____
0 name: _____   0 name: _____
   because: _____   because: _____
   _____   _____
   _____   _____
   _____   _____
   _____   _____

Section VIII Summary

Tests 38, 39, and 40 assess the interests of the students in the primary, intermediate and upper grades. These measures help the teacher to select library books for the classroom. Because interests change they may be given as many times as needed.

Tests 41 and 42 measure attitude towards reading. Test 42 is recommended for longitudinal studies because it is a wide-range test. Since the test is also self-anchoring it allows the researcher to categorize changes in students' values and attitudes over the years.

References

Cantril, Hadley, and Lloyd Free, "Hopes and Fears for Self and Country." *American Behavioral Scientist,* Vol. 6 (Supplement, Oct.), p. 8.

Mager, Robert F. *Developing Attitude Toward Learning.* Palo Alto, Ca.: Fearon Publishers, 1968, pp. 31-38.

appendices

language dominance cards
English/Spanish

These cards are to be used with Test 10. They are coded as follows:

I-I	7-II	13-III	19-IV	25-V	31-VI
2-I	8-II	14-III	20-IV	26-V	32-VI
3-I	9-II	15-III	21-IV	27-V	33-VI
4-I	10-II	16-III	22-IV	28-V	34-VI
5-I	11-II	17-III	23-IV	29-V	35-VI
6-I	12-II	18-III	24-IV	30-V	36-VI

Reproduce the 36 cards and band them together in groups of 6.

1 -I

2 -I

3 -I

4 -I

5 -I

6 -I

¿Qué color?

7 -II

8 -II

9 -II

¿Qué color?

10 -II

11 -II

12 -II

25-V

26-V

27-V

28-V

29-V

30-V

31-VI

32-VI

33-VI

34-VI

35-VI

36-VI

san diego quick assessment cards

Form I

These cards are to be used with Test 11. They are coded as follows:

I-RR[1]	I-2	I-6	I-10
I-RR[2]	I-3	I-7	I-11
I-RR[3]	I-4	I-8	I-12
I-1	I-5	I-9	I-13

Reproduce these 16 cards and place them in a photographic album so that they can be flipped over as completed. Sequence them in this order: RR[1], RR[2], RR[3], I-1 through I-13.

I-RR²

B
A
M
C
S
J
T
H
D
W

I-1

see
play
me
at
run
go
and
look
can
here

I-RR¹

B B
A C
M M
C C
S Q
J J
T T
H H
D L
W M

I-RR³

D B A
A E K
L F M
B C G
O S P
A B J
D G T
A H B
D I M
W G J

I-3

road
live
thank
when
bigger
how
always
night
spring
today

I-5

city
middle
moment
frightened
exclaimed
several
lonely
drew
since
straight

I-2

you
come
not
with
jump
help
is
work
are
this

I-4

our
please
myself
town
early
send
wide
believe
quietly
carefully

I-6

decided
served
amazed
silent
wrecked
improve
certainly
entered
realized
interrupted

I-7

scanty
business
develop
considered
discussed
behaved
splendid
acquainted
escape
grim

I-8

bridge
commercial
abolish
trucker
apparatus
elementary
comment
necessity
gallery
relativity

I-9

amber
dominion
sundry
capillary
impetuous
blight
wrest
enumerate
daunted
condescend

I-10

capacious
limitations
pretext
intrigue
delusions
immaculate
ascent
acrid
binoculars
embankment

I-11

conscientious
isolation
molecule
ritual
momentous
vulnerable
kinship
conservatism
jaunty
inventive

I-12

zany
jerkin
nausea
gratuitous
linear
inept
legality
aspen
amnesty
barometer

I-13

galore
rotunda
capitalism
prevaricate
risible
exonerate
superannuate
luxuriate
piebald
crunch

san diego quick assessment cards
Form II

These cards are to be used with Test 12. They are coded as follows:

II-RR^1	II-2	II-6	II-10
II-RR^2	II-3	II-7	II-11
II-RR^3	II-4	II-8	II-12
II-1	II-5	II-9	II-13

Reproduce these 16 cards and place them in a photographic album so that they can be flipped over as completed. Sequence them in this order: RR^1, RR^2, RR^3, II-1 through II-13.

II-RR²

```
D
K
N
B
J
L
W
Y
A
F

C L
```

II-1

```
red
jump
be
it
ran
come
to
I
ride
book
```

II-RR¹

```
H  L
A  A
N  M
D  D
S  L
W  M
F  F
D  B
K  K
Y  Y
```

II-RR³

```
A  L  D
K  L  M
W  N  G
B  D  M
C  L  J
F  L  N
A  W  E
H  O  Y
A  H  B
F  E  Q
```

load
give
bank
ten
from
now
almost
winter
Monday
white

cent
riddles
movement
light
reclaim
grade
alone
few
already
eight

he
want
no
the
find
home
will
too
was
them

your
track
herself
dance
ear
back
dark
received
quiet
bravely

II-7

shape
blaze
defeated
consider
distress
bicycle
splendor
acquired
escort
interplay

II-9

torment
provision
dainty
stationary
frontier
flight
wrist
ambitious
marsh
descend

II-6

reside
curves
famous
violent
wrong
important
surely
centered
returned
science

II-8

breach
financial
polished
lucky
crimes
opposite
lament
security
notable
ignorance

II-10

alfalfa
savor
biscuits
contrary
deign
firmament
gymnasium
insanity
flaunted
protoplasm

II-11

concentrate
immunity
secondary
crevice
cascade
spur
reverberate
solitary
lulled
fanatical

II-12

trance
enterprise
querulous
interval
technique
vegetarian
replenishing
obscurely
compulsion
verbatim

II-13

recumbent
ominously
diminishing
soliloquy
incandescence
meditations
deprecating
provender
terrapins
terminate

255

san diego quick oral paragraphs

Form 1

These cards are to be used with Test 32. They are coded as follows:

1-1	(Preprimer)	1-6	(Fourth)
1-2	(Primer)	1-7	(Fifth)
1-3	(First)	1-8	(Sixth)
1-4	(Second)	1-9	(Seventh)
1-5	(Third)	1-10	(Eighth)

Reproduce the 10 cards, punch holes on the left side, and place them on loose leaf rings in the correct sequence.

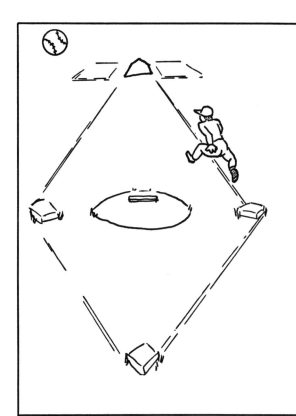

See me play ball.
I can run.
Look at me go.
I can run and play here.
Look at me run home.

I-1

Come and jump in with me. This boat is fun.
You can help me sail. It is not work to sail.
We are in a sailboat.

I-2

Today is spring. When spring is here, I like to fish.

I live by a road. I walk on this road when I want to fish. How the day flies by. I always try for a bigger and bigger fish.

If I get a big one, Mom will thank me. We will eat it this night.

I-3

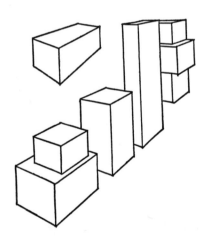

I made this block town to please myself. I got up early and worked quietly. I made a wide road. Then, I carefully put block on block. I believe it will not fall down.

Our house is quiet today. I am working quietly and carefully. Mother will not send me out to play.

I-4

The boy looked frightened. He was in the middle of the walk. He looked lonely in the city as the cars zoomed by.

In a moment, several men walked past.

A tall man drew up in a car. He got out and walked straight to the boy. "Why aren't you in school?" The man exclaimed.

Since the boy did not know what to say, he began to cry.

I-5

A boy decided to improve the car he was making. It was not a silent car, but it served him well. It certainly wasn't a racing car, but going downhill it was fast.

The boy entered a downhill race. He realized his car was not a race car. Still he wanted to try.

On the day of the race, his car amazed him, and he was pleased. It went so fast downhill, he might have won, but the race was interrupted. His car hit a rock and was wrecked.

I-6

The three boys were tied up as a Halloween trick by a badly behaved gang.
"Something will develop," one of the boys said, as they discussed how to escape.
"We have a scanty chance," another boy said sadly.
"I've escaped from other tie-ups," said the smallest boy. But no one listened.
"Have you considered how grim it would be to be tied up all night?" The fattest boy said. "This business of missing all the spendid Halloween treats is no fun."
The smallest boy said, "If you were acquainted with Boy Scout knots, you could get out of this."
This time someone listened. "Okay, smarty. Get us out."
And the smallest boy did.

I-7

The girls were told to make up a new city in a make-believe land by using any apparatus. They floated a bridge on a cushion of air, and in their land, a trucker is able to cross a bridge by putting up a wind sail. The sails abolish pollution from all cars, and commercial factories have giant wind mills for power. The necessity of storing wind for quiet times is great. A new idea about relativity was formed. It was not as elementary as the old ideas.

In the make-believe land, an art gallery is made up of moving forms. People comment on the beauty of motion.

I-8

Americans celebrate the Fourth of July, but Canadians celebrate July first. They celebrate what they call the Dominion of Canada Day. This is in honor of the Union of Canada under one government. There are too many provinces in the dominion to enumerate them. Dominions remain loyal to England.

Some Canadians speak English and some speak French. Americans visiting Canada are daunted by their own inability to speak French when they see very young children speaking the language rapidly. Bookstands advertise various and sundry dictionaries of common words to help wrest meaning out of what is heard. Impetuous Americans dare to try their high school French on sales clerks while shy Americans remain quiet.

Some French words are easy to learn. The word for amber, the yellowish brown color, is "ambre" in French. The reason the words are so similar is that amber comes from the French language. In tracing the origin of words there is much branching or capillary action. Such words as amberoid, synthetic amber and ambergris, used in perfume, are branches of the word amber.

To get back to the Canadians and their language, the French-Canadians appreciate having visitors try to speak their language. They consider it a blight on America that so few Americans can speak more than one language. As you shop in a French-Canadian store the clerks will condescend to wait on English-speaking customers. They give more attention, however, as a usual practice, to those who make an attempt to speak the native tongue. They are pleased with those visitors who try to express themselves in the tongue of the country they are visiting.

I-9

A large building rose above the already high embankment. To give you some idea of the size of the building you could see it from five miles away — without binoculars. Some people say that the owner had delusions of grandeur. Others say he wanted to become the richest man in the world. He built with no limitations as to budget. Whatever his pretext was for building such a huge building, everyone agreed it was the largest in all of North America.

Every detail of the structure and grounds was elegant. The ascent to the embankment was built with spacious steps. Gardens around the building were immaculate and well kept. Inside the rooms were capacious with wide corridors as well as large rooms. The living room was large enough for a fleet of cars to be stored.

How the owner ever amassed enough money to build such a structure no one was ever able to figure out. Lots of talk of intrigue surrounded his life, particularly his finances. People with acrid tongues said he robbed banks. A more logical explanation would be that a relative had died leaving him a fortune. But no matter what the source, the owner evidently wanted a monument that would be long associated with his name.

I-10

san diego quick oral paragraphs

Form II

These cards are to be used with Test 33. They are coded as follows:

II-1	(Preprimer)	II-6	(Fourth)
II-2	(Primer)	II-7	(Fifth)
II-3	(First)	II-8	(Sixth)
II-4	(Second)	II-9	(Seventh)
II-5	(Third)	II-10	(Eighth)

Reproduce the 10 cards, punch holes on the left side, and place them on loose leaf rings in the correct sequence.

"Come here.
See.
Ride and Jump is my book."

I ran to see it.
"It is red.
It looks like my book
Can it be my book?"

"He wants a book.
Is this the book?"

"No. It was red.
I want to find one, too.
We will take them home.
We like books."

Now it is winter. Almost any day there will be lots of white snow. Maybe by Monday we will have a load of snow. I hope so. Last winter snow banks were high.

From the snow, I will make ten snowballs. I will give you five. Then look out. I could snowball you.

II-3

Ann was a fast runner. She wanted to be on the track team. One day she fell.
"She hurt herself," another girl said.
"No, I didn't," Ann said. She got up bravely.
"Your ear is dark red," her friend said. "You received quite a bad fall."
"I'm okay," Ann said. "I want to be back at school for the May dance."
"We will see," said her friend.

II-4

One boy went to reclaim his third grade book. He came back to his eight friends who were telling riddles. A few boys could not think of any.

One boy made a movement as if to go.

"Don't go," the other boys said. "We already have a good one for you."

"What makes you think of a skunk? It begins with a 'C.' It is another way of saying penny."

"A cent," one boy shouted all alone.

"Okay, I get it. I see the light," another boy said.

II-5

Science is becoming more important these days than it used to be. Many scientists reside near their work. Many new things are centered around science. Push button dialing is new. Change is returned to you in stores by machine. TV is a famous invention. Surely we live in a great age.

Science thows us curves too. Not all that it does is for our good. It invents some violent things, such as guns and bombs. Many of these things can be used in the wrong way.

II-6

I acquired a second-hand bicycle but there was too much interplay between the parts. I had planned to race it, but I was in distress. The wheels wobbled and the chains banged. I felt defeated.

Should I consider reselling it? No. I thought that I could put it in shape. I worked hard to make everything fit. Then I polished it until it shone in a blaze of spendor. It was beautiful enough to escort the winner of a race.

II-7

Banks and loan centers are notable buildings of marble and polished metals. They are concerned with financial dealings, opposite in nature. Both are interested in money "taken in" and in money "going out." Both need tight security. Bank clerks who commit a breach of trust cause bankers to lament and to get more security. Banks that are free of all such crimes are lucky. Crimes of ignorance are forgivable but not those of theft.

II-8

The writer was in a torment. It was two years since he had sold his last book. He had made no provision for so long a time without any income. He was a small man with a dainty appetite but even so, he was beginning to be hungry.

As a young boy he had been ambitious. He wrote well, and would walk in the marsh thinking of new stories. His mind would take flight especially in spinning tales about frontier days. Then he would descend to his basement den where he had a large stationary desk. He would write there until his wrist ached.

II-9

No teacher would deign to teach health in our school in any room but the big gymnasium. Contrary to conditions in some schools the subject was one of our most popular. Our students flaunted their knowledge of such things as definitions of protoplasm, kinds of insanity, and the importance of good nutrition. Most came to feel that diet is the great sun in the firmament of health, and they began to savor alfalfa sprouts, and all vegetables and fruits. They even, in many cases, preferred them to biscuits and pastries.

II-10